Cap-and-Tı

CW01082559

versus Carbo

Carbon Pricing Issues and Selected Country Implementations

1st Edition, October 2022

Disclosure

A shorter and older version of this book was published with the title "Cap and Trade and Carbon Credits: An Introduction to Carbon Trading"

Contents

What is Cap-and-Trade?

Definition

Cap-and-Trade is the free market approach to limiting pollutants in the air.

When companies are rewarded to emit less than a maximum amount of pollutants (i.e., "the cap"), they are expected to repeat the "clean behavior" and emit less pollutants, according to the liberal theory of market economy.

Conversely, when they are penalized for going over the cap, they are expected either to lessen their emissions or purchase the right to do so (i.e., "trade") from those who keep their emissions below the cap.

This scheme is expected to act as a self-regulating mechanism to keep emissions in check and even decrease it over the long run.

How it works

Both the private sector and the U.S. Congress are wrangling over the same scheme that is supposed to stop and hopefully reverse global warming - the "cap-and-trade" system of "carbon credits."

This is how the scheme works:

Carbon dioxide (CO_2) is known to be the number one polluter of our atmosphere and thus number one culprit in global warming. Private companies, and especially utility companies that produce energy through fossil fuels like coal, are among the top producers of CO_2. In the past, there had been no limits to the amount of CO_2 that such companies could produce.

Thus, someone suggested to create an artificial "scarcity" of CO_2, which would be a very good thing.

How do you do that? By passing a law to limit the amount of CO_2 that each company can produce.

But what if a company produces LESS than its allowed amount? Or what if another company decides to produce MORE carbon dioxide for various reasons?

Then the company that's below its "carbon emission quota" is allowed to sell that "right to pollute" on the open market to the company that needs it to emit more carbon into the atmosphere. Thus, such "carbon permits" can be sold and bought just like regular stocks in the stock market.

The cap-and-trade system is already in use in Europe since March 2007 and the prices of such permits tripled within the first few years of their introduction (but fell sharply afterwards). As explained later in this report, the situation has reversed in 2011 with stiff political opposition and dropping credit trading volumes in major European energy exchanges.

The fight for and against carbon credits and cap-and-trade scheme is a dynamic one with positions and allegiances won and lost almost on a monthly basis. That's why we try to update this book annually to reflect the latest developments in the field.

An increasing number of giant corporations in the U.S. are now endorsing the cap-and-trade system believing they need to be at the table when the nature and amount of such caps are decided. The thinking is, you either have a role in determining the rules of the cap-and-trade game or you live by its ramifications. You are either sitting at the steering wheel of this cap-and-trade juggernaut or you are going to get hit by it. But as we said earlier, the resistance to cap-and-trade grew throughout 2011 with occasional "victories" here and there like California's adoption of an official cap-and-trade program in October 2011.

A Key Assumption

A key assumption worth mentioning which underlies all the cap-and-trade discussions is this: the trend for global warming might still be manageable if the warming of our planet is limited to **a maximum of two-degrees Celsius [3.6°F].** And to accomplish that, there needs to be a cap on and reduction of greenhouse gas emissions starting in **2020** the latest.

SOURCE:

https://www.worldbank.org/en/programs/pricing-carbon

Alternative to Cap-and-Trade:
Carbon Tax

S ome observers and economists suggested "carbon tax" (or an "emission fee") as an alternative to the cap-and-trade scheme. It is levied not only on emissions of CO2, but methane, nitrous oxide, and fluorinated gases as well.

The initiative, which was taken seriously in a number of English-speaking countries like the United States, England, and Australia, has yielded mixed results.

In EU (and as of 2022), the carbon tax is lowest in Poland (€ 0.07 per ton) and Ukraine (€ 0.93 per ton), and highest in Sweden, Liechtenstein, and Switzerland (€ 117).

In California, carbon tax is considered by some as a viable alternative to the cap-and-trade scheme which has been handicapped by fierce and increasing Republican opposition (like in New Jersey).

Carbon tax is a tax on the carbon content of fossil fuels (coal, oil, gas). It's about levying a monetary penalty on those industries that produce carbon dioxide (CO_2) as a result of burning carbon-based fuels. While cap-and-trade scheme provides an incentive for those companies to produce green-house gases (of which CO_2 is one) who can afford it by purchasing carbon credits, **carbon tax idea tries to prevent CO2 release in the first place.**

The idea of a "carbon tax" has gained so much traction that in year 2007 a **Carbon Tax Center** was founded in Washington D.C. (http://www.carbontax.org/).

According to the **Carbon Tax Center (CTC)**, a carbon tax is the most economically efficient means to convey crucial price signals and spur carbon-reducing investment. It is necessary, the CTC claims, since the cap-and-trade scheme with offsets cannot deliver the needed emissions reductions. See the YouTube video, "The Huge Mistake": http://www.youtube.com/watch?v=BA-QufQzuWU

The issue was a hot bone of contention in the United States as of 2011 between those who favor President Obama's support for cap-and-trade (mainly environmentalists and Democrats) and those who oppose it (mainly conservatives and Republicans). Yet despite the political opposition, cap-and-trade still survived its critics in California when California Air Resources Board announced that, when compared to other alternatives, cap-and-trade still looked like a viable solution. California has passed a mandate to pull the green-house gas emission levels by 2020 back to where they were back in 1990.

In Britain, the country's largest business lobby CBI has come out strongly against carbon tax. "The CBI supports the carbon floor price in principle, but we have to see exemptions for those industries most at risk - those very industries that are a critical part of our low-carbon economy," said the CBI's director general, John Cridland.

Among the U.S. supporters of the carbon tax idea were New York City mayor Michael Bloomberg and the U.S. Congressional Budget Office.

How do they compare?

Brookins Institution said "A carbon tax and cap-and-trade are opposite sides of the same coin. A carbon tax sets the price of carbon dioxide emissions and allows the market to determine the quantity of emission reductions. Cap-and-trade sets the quantity of emissions reductions and lets the market determine the price."

You either set

•   **The unit price of CO2 emission** and then let the market decide the amount of CO2 to be released, or

•   **The amount of CO2** to be released and then let the market decide on the unit price of CO2 to be released.

These two alternatives have different advantages and disadvantages, depending on the issue and the context.

•   **A compromise solution**. Some observers suggested **a "hedging" strategy** since in some contexts there is no clear-cut formula by which to tell which alternative is better. In many cases it's hard to decide whether the cap-and-trade or the carbon tax scheme is better to limit the emission of greenhouse gases like CO2. Thus, as a compromise, they suggest governments should establish a "**safety valve price**" by which the companies that reach the emission cap can purchase permits to pollute more.

•   **Inflation** – Cap-and-trade adjusts itself automatically for inflation. Carbon tax or emission fees need to be adjusted separately.

•   **Allowances** – Cap-and-trade require allowances for acceptable levels of emissions. That brings an additional administrative load to the equation. Especially when it comes to automobile transportation or residential heating and cooling, setting allowances will prove to be very difficult indeed. Carbon tax, on the other hand, does not have that administrative requirement. However, cap-and-trade can still be adopted with minimal administrative overlay in selected sectors by auctioning the allowances, as done by nine eastern U.S. states comprising the Regional Greenhouse Gas Initiative (RGGI).

SOURCES:

https://www.brookings.edu/blog/planetpolicy/2014/08/12/pricing-carbon-a-carbon-tax-or-cap-and-trade/

https://taxfoundation.org/carbon-taxes-in-europe-2022/

https://www.worldbank.org/en/programs/pricing-carbon

NOTES

Issues with Cap-and-Trade

The cap-and-trade system envisions allocating certain carbon emission quotas for different firms and then allowing them to buy and sell their permits on a stock-market platform.

It is assumed that the cost of buying extra permits and continuing to pollute the atmosphere will at some point be so prohibitive that most companies will simply prefer to cut down their CO_2 emissions and invest in cleaner fuel technologies.

There are still quite a few issues for this system to work properly.

(1) The world is still very dependent on carbon-based fuels. Eighty percent of world production relies on technologies that release carbon into the atmosphere. So even if carbon credits were bought and sold widely in an open market, unless more funds were channeled into alternative and clean technologies, consumers will end up paying more for everything they buy. A cap on carbon production ceiling is not a cap on consumer prices. Thus, from a strictly pocket-book point of view, the resistance to such a scheme will continue to grow on the part of the consuming public.

(2) This brings us to the second built-in issue: the political problem. There aren't too many politicians who can win an election by disclosing the hidden costs of limiting the "carbon footprint." Would the voters be willing to face skyrocketing consumer prices or brownouts and blackouts? How would they express their grievance at election time?

(3) Third issue involves the way in which the caps themselves are defined.

For example, would the same numeric cap make sense for a coal-fired utility company and a nuclear-based energy company? The minute you vote on a fixed percentage of CO_2 released, you would be putting the coal-utility at a distinct disadvantage.

You might argue that that is precisely the idea - to squeeze and steer the worst offenders towards clean technologies. But when such alternative technologies do not yet exist, such a decision would be tantamount to a death knell for some quite powerful concerns and it's clear that they will not go down quietly into the night without putting up a fight first.

So we'll see a lot of political pushing and shoving in the years ahead on this issue from different interest groups and industry lobbies.

(4) There is no price stability in carbon trading. It all depends on the carbon price that the market supports, which changes day to day and month to month. Thus investors, planners, and innovators have difficulty in planning for the future.

Issues with Carbon Tax

Finland was the first country in the world to introduce a carbon tax in 1990 to control emissions. That was followed by 19 more EU countries.

As of 2022, the carbon tax in EU varies between € 1 per ton (Poland and Ukraine) to € 100 (Sweden, Liechtenstein, Switzerland).

(1) Tax is a negative word. No politician, administrator, or voter wants to hear about a new tax. There is a considerable political price to pay for defending the carbon tax in public.

(2) But on the other hand, carbon tax represents a fixed emission price. That kind of price certainty can encourage innovation and new clean technologies.

(3) Revenue collected from a carbon tax is collected by a central government agency which, in theory, may encourage efficient spending for a variety of different purposes.

(4) Carbon tax needs to be adjusted periodically to align it with emission goals and that represents an additional administrative load for the governments.

SOURCES:

https://www.imf.org/-/media/Files/Publications/Staff-Climate-Notes/2022/English/CLNEA2022006.ashx

https://taxfoundation.org/carbon-taxes-in-europe-2022/

IMF: Emissions are Still Too Cheap

IMF in 2022 issued a warning on climate change with the title "More Countries Are Pricing Carbon, but Emissions Are Still Too Cheap."

The emission controls and carbon tax together cover only 30% of emissions globally, with carbon tax as high as $90 per ton in EU.

IMF recommends raising carbon taxes from its 2022 average of $9 per ton of CO2 to $75 by 2030. In some EU countries like Sweden, Switzerland and Lichenstein the tax is already about $110. Thus it's clear that no progress can be made on the pricing front without the participation of big emitters like the United States, China, Russia, and India.

However, IMF admits that "countries may choose different approaches based on their own circumstances and objectives," a fact which complicates the picture immediately.

Capping and trading emission levels creates certainty about future emission levels which is preferred by policy makers and investors. Carbon tax, on the other hand, is simple to implement (like as an add-on to the existing fuel tax) and provide more certainty about future financial planning (even though it's a political hot potato).

But all schemes, regardless of their differences, are based on the "polluter pays" principle which will continue to be a sound concept to work with in the future.

SOURCE:

https://www.imf.org/en/Blogs/Articles/2022/07/21/blog-more-countries-are-pricing-carbon-but-emissions-are-still-too-cheap

2022 IMF Study

I MF has released an excellent study in 2022 comparing various advantages and disadvantages of cap-and-trade and carbon taxing.

Ian Parry, Simon Black, and Karlygash Zhunussova. 2022. "Carbon Taxes or Emissions Trading Systems? Instrument Choice and Design" IMF Staff Climate Note 2022/006, International Monetary Fund, Washington, DC.

The study is jampacked with data and easy-to-understand graphics that summarize the relative merits of different carbon pricing schemes.

Why Carbon Pricing?

The study starts with the rationale for having any carbon pricing system at all.

The driving necessity of curbing GHGs comes from the fact that the GHG emissions need to be reduced by 25 to 50 percent until 2030 if we are to succeed in containing global warming to 1.5 to 2 degrees centigrade. Anything above 2° C may trigger irreversible environmental catastrophes, according to many scientists.

Avoiding a global catastrophe… That's the backbone rationale for carbon pricing (any form of it) since making carbon emissions expensive seems to be the only way to curb their release given the fact that no other method has been proven to be effective or feasible so far. That's why 130 countries, producing 90% of GHGs, have proposed to reach zero net emissions by 2050.

In this study IMF recommends that "gradually raising fossil fuel prices through carbon pricing should be the centerpiece of countries' mitigation strategies."

We can summarize the good reasons for carbon pricing under three headings:

• **Emissions reductions.** Levying a price on carbon emissions do reduce energy use and encourage a shift to lower-carbon fuels.
• **Investment and innovation for clean energy.** Carbon pricing encourages the development of innovative technologies like green energy or better scrubbing systems. The rate of innovation is directly proportional to the credibility of continuing (and perhaps rising) price of carbon emissions.
• **Increased revenues.** Governments enjoy increased revenues thanks to carbon pricing which can support worthwhile social and development targets.

Countries with Carbon Pricing

As of 2022, the following countries have established carbon pricing either through carbon taxing and/or some other kind of carbon trading policy:

- Canada — $15-to-$30 **per metric ton of CO2**

- Britain — $25

- United States — $5 (9 Northeastern states), $15 (California)

- Australia — $10

- Mexico

- Colombia

- Chile

- Argentina

- Iceland

- Sweden (€ 117 per metric ton)

- Norway

- European Union

- Switzerland (€ 117 per metric ton)

- Lichenstein (€ 117 per metric ton)

- Ukraine (€ 0.93 per metric ton)

- Kazakhstan

- Japan

- New Zealand

- Poland (€ 0.07 per metric ton)

SOURCES:

https://www.nytimes.com/interactive/2019/04/02/climate/pricing-carbon-emissions.html?action=click&module=RelatedLinks&pgtype=Article

https://taxfoundation.org/carbon-taxes-in-europe-2022/

https://www.statista.com/statistics/483590/prices-of-implemented-carbon-pricing-instruments-worldwide-by-select-country/

https://www.imf.org/en/Blogs/Articles/2022/07/21/blog-more-countries-are-pricing-carbon-but-emissions-are-still-too-cheap

American Clean Energy and Security Act of 2009

The legal basis of cap-and-trade in the United States is provided by **American Clean Energy and Security Act (ACES)** of 2009, Bill # H.R.2454 which is also known as the **"Waxman-Markey Cap and Trade Bill."** See: http://www.govtrack.us/congress/bill.xpd?bill=h111-2454

H.R.2454 introduced a cap-and-trade system that will affect all American taxpayers.

The U.S. government is mandated to set an upper limit to the total amount of greenhouse gases that can be released in a year, nationally. It also redefined U.S. federal renewable electric energy standards which some observers predict will raise the utility prices.

The utility companies are required to acquire 20% of their energy needs from renewable sources by the year 2020. The bill also introduces subsidies for renewable energy sectors ($90 bn by 2025) and incentives for new technologies like electric cars ($20 bn), carbon capture and sequestration ($60 bn), and scientific research and development ($20 bn).

At the consumer level, the bill ushers in new electricity consumption requirements for a number of consumer and household appliances including jacuzzis, water dispensers, commercial food warmers, outdoor flood lamps, and indoor house lamps.

Here is a criticism of the 2009 bill (YouTube video):

http://www.youtube.com/watch?v=BA-QufQzuWU

ACES was voted down by the U.S. Senate.

See APPENDIX: *Support for and Opposition to H.R. 2454*

2019 Economists' Statement on Carbon Dividends

On January 17, 2019, The Wall Street Journal has published "The Largest Public Statement of Economists in History" (https://clcouncil.org/economists-statement/) and also **the strongest public endorsement of the carbon tax idea to date** by an impressive group of thought leaders.

This short but clear statement was signed by

- 3623 U.S. economists

- 4 former chairs of U.S. Federal Reserve

- 28 Nobel Laureate economists

- 15 former chairs of U.S. Council of Economic Advisers

This is as impressive a group of economists and scientists as you'll ever get.

And this is what they said in the first article of their five-article policy recommendation statement:

"A **carbon tax** offers the most cost-effective lever to reduce carbon emissions at the scale and speed that is necessary. By correcting a well-known market failure, a carbon tax will send a powerful price signal that harnesses the invisible hand of the marketplace to steer economic actors towards a low-carbon future."

But has this carbon tax recommendation been followed by the U.S. government?

We have to look (next) at one of the most important legislation the Biden Administration managed to steer through the U.S. Congress in a rare example of bipartisanship: **The 2022 Inflation Reduction Act.**

Problem of "Data Deficit"

Everybody would love to live in a zero-net-emission world. But how are we going to measure emission levels? Unless we have reliable data measurement units and techniques that can be applied, enforced, and checked objectively across international boundaries, stakeholders and policymakers can never agree on anything.

The need for reliable data is obvious. **IMF**, however, has concluded in 2022 that currently "financial market participants face a lack of high-quality, reliable, and comparable data needed to efficiently price climate related risks and avoid greenwashing— spurious attempts by financial or non-financial companies to burnish their environmental credentials." (See the Source below).

The **Network for Greening the Financial System (NGFS)**, issued an important report about bridging the data gaps (see the Sources), a study supported by IMF and the European Central Bank.

The report's major contribution is its proposal for a **Climate-Data Directory**, a survey of available data and how it is used globally.

The report highlighted three main findings:

- Insufficient data in disclosures of non-publicly listed companies and small and medium-sized companies

- Limited availability of comparable and science-based forward-looking data, such as targets, commitments, and emissions pathways

- Limited audits that's necessary to build trust in the system

NGFS report noted that the following data is missing:

"Missing are accounting data and exact geographic location of assets, as well as data on greenhouse-gas emissions and effects related to biodiversity, forest depletion, floods, droughts, and storms."

SOURCES:

https://www.imf.org/en/Blogs/Articles/2022/08/23/achieving-net-zero-emissions-requires-closing-a-data-deficit

https://www.ngfs.net/en/final-report-bridging-data-gaps

2022 Inflation Reduction Act (IRA)

Even though its title does not mention "carbon tax" or "cap-and-trade," this is a major legislation aimed at reducing global warming and expanding the alternative energy sector like solar and wind power.

The section of the act addressing energy and climate change focuses on "creating clean energy jobs" without any mention of harder policy measures like a carbon tax.

The recommended policy measures in IRA include:

• Expanding tax credits for energy-efficient homes…

• Tax credits for electric vehicle (EV) purchase and charging stations…

• Support for nuclear energy plants…

• "Clean energy tax credits for wind, solar, nuclear, clean hydrogen, clean fuels, and carbon capture…"

•   Making sure workers in clean-energy sectors are trained and paid competitively…

But there is nothing explicit in IRA supporting the idea of a carbon tax or cap-and-trade scheme. Yes, the act supports "carbon sequestration" but that would not prevent usage of fossil fuels.

As Forbes has noted, "Rather than implementing a carbon tax, the administration has decided to expand several clean energy tax credit programs and offer new tax credits."

In his analysis "**Why We Don't Have a Carbon Tax**," **Paul Krugman** (distinguished professor in the Graduate Center Economics Ph.D. program and distinguished scholar at the Luxembourg Income Study Center at the City University of New York) said the act "doesn't include a carbon tax, nor does it introduce a system of tradable emissions permits, which would provide similar incentives."

As Krugman underlines, it all comes down to two choices to counter and reduce the emission of greenhouse gases like CO2:

•   Let the market do its presumed magic and establish a balance between the cost and corporate benefits of doing business as usual, or

•   Adopt an explicit industrial policy that defines that cost in terms of a carbon tax or a policy to similar effect.

In this discussion, there is a third and key factor to consider: the **cost and type of new alternative technologies** developed. Government incentives and subsidies are clearly involved in the development of such technologies. That means there will also be a **political component** to all the variables in the equation which makes the defense of a carbon tax or cap-and-trade policy even more intricate.

"Beyond the straight economics, there are overwhelming political arguments against making carbon taxes the centerpiece of climate policy," as Krugman notes. Allergy to any new taxes (regardless of what's done with such new revenue) and dread of "big government" are two such political concerns raised as a matter of principle by the Republicans in the U.S. which the Democrats must and do consider.

That's why a successful climate control bill has to be a "**Christmas tree**," Krugman notes, adorned with gifts for all interests and parties in order to overcome political rejection. IRA is one such Christmas tree legislation even though it has no room for a simple and straightforward carbon tax in it.

SOURCES:

https://www.npr.org/2022/08/21/1118669854/the-inflation-reduction-act-incentivizes-capturing-carbon-emissions

https://www.accountingtoday.com/news/does-the-inflation-reduction-act-contain-a-carbon-tax

https://www.forbes.com/sites/taxnotes/2022/08/25/carrot-vs-stick-the-inflation-reduction-acts-energy-tax-provisions/?sh=14fa4f3e3369

https://www.nytimes.com/2022/08/16/opinion/carbon-tax.html

State-Level Opposition in USA

T he opposition to cap-and-trade has been stiff at the local level in the United States. Since the first time the idea was aired, cap-and-trade has become a sort of "political football" between those Democrats strongly backing it and the Republicans opposing it with same vigor.

Politicians like Mass. Senator John Kerry (a Democrat), who went on the record saying "I don't know what 'cap-and-trade ' means" is one of the few exceptions to the rule. Sen. Lindsey Graham, for example, a South Carolina Republican, has announced cap-and-trade "dead" in 2011.

The future of **Regional Greenhouse Gas Initiative**, or RGGI (http://rggi.org/docs/mou_final_12_20_05.pdf), signed in 2008, for example, is in doubt after New Jersey pulled out of the regional cap-and-trade arrangement that was supposed to regulate carbon emissions in 10 Northeastern states. New Jersey Gov. Chris Christie announced in June 2011 that the Garden State is bailing out. NJ will leave RGGI at the end of 2011. The decision was made on the basis of this report (http://www.state.nj.us/dep/newsrel/2011/11_0069.htm) which claimed that the state was already ahead of its 2020 emission target, thus making the RGGI unnecessary.

While the Democrats always stress "leaving a clean environment for our children", the Republican angle focuses on economics and the pocketbook, claiming cap-and-trade schemes end up increasing the cost of electricity production without any clear environmental benefits. The Republican skepticism towards the related issue of "Global Warming" bolsters their anti cap-and-trade position.

Carbon Credit Trading is the New "Derivatives" Game

Technically speaking, "carbon credits" (CC) are not true "derivatives" of course since, unlike stock options, they do not have an "underlying asset" or "instrument."

A "carbon credit" is basically the "right to pollute" sold by those less-polluting companies to those who do not, for one reason or another, want to curb their carbon dioxide emissions yet. Their prices probably rely more on the laws passed by legislative bodies in respective parliaments than on net corporate worth, any technical ratios or interest rates.

The market to buy and sell such credits is especially hot in Europe where most countries have signed the U.N. Kyoto Protocol to curb CO_2 emissions. The United States still has not signed the Protocol.

Since to sell these credits as individual companies you need to register your energy-saving and carbon-suppressing projects with the United Nations and get U.N. certification, the U.S. companies cannot yet do that directly. That's why London is right now the busy hub of the $25 billion carbon credit trading market where 60% of all transactions take place - compared to only 10% in the U.S.

However, the U.S. investors already do participate in this new exciting market through various hedge funds that play at the 200-member Chicago Climate Exchange, Inc.

The pressures to sign the Kyoto Protocol and to participate more directly in the world-wide carbon credit trade comes from major states like California.

Former Gov. Arnold Schwarzenegger has signed in September 2006 a law that mandates cutting down the CA carbon emissions by 25% as of 2020. This would of course increase the attention paid to CC trading as well since it is a lucrative way to self-finance many alternative energy projects.

A major development to spur Washington in that direction would be the launching of a carbon credit exchange soon in Beijing, China. In a related development, Industrial Bank and China Beijing Environment Exchange have jointly launched a "low-carbon credit card" in 2011. The press announcement introduced the card in Beijing as "China's first low-carbon credit card". It is welcomed as a major tool to encourage the average Chinese citizens to save energy and reduce emissions.

With China joining the carbon credit market at the consumer level, we might be witnessing only the beginning of a brand new trading sector that will make itself felt strongly in the months and years ahead.

Carbon Credit "Manufacturing" - A New Industrial Growth Sector

D id you know that companies can now buy and sell "carbon credits" internationally just like other goods and services regularly bought and sold on the international market?

There are two important prerequisites for this new carbon credit business:

1) Your country must have signed the Kyoto Protocol of 2005 (the United States has still not signed it). These credits are made possible by the Kyoto's Clean Development Mechanism (CDM). That's why sometimes this new line of trading is also referred to simply as "CDM" business.

2) You have to register your "carbon saving" project with the United Nations before you can sell your credits to other international purchasers.

India's leading energy company "Oil and Natural Gas Corp" did exactly that. ONGC expects to sell 850,000 tons worth of "carbon credits" (that is, the right to release that much carbon dioxide into the atmosphere) for Rs 600 million - or RS 705 per ton.

Some studies suggest, for example, that the total "carbon credit potential" of forests in New Zealand can add up to $13,000 to $20,000 per hectare over the life of the forest. Why? Because trees remove carbon dioxide from the atmosphere.

Who knew the "right to pollute" could be this lucrative a growth market?

So who buys these carbon credits? Western companies from countries that have signed the Kyoto Protocol who for one reason or another either cannot or do not want to reduce their carbon emissions. Such companies find it cheaper to buy the right to release CO2 from more efficient companies in the developing world like ONGC. The Indian giant has announced it will register 11 energy saving projects to reduce gas flaring with the United Nations by the end of 2007. That will of course translate to new authorization to sell more carbon credits and more revenues for ONGC for reducing its CO2 emissions.

Projects to reduce wasted heat in industrial plants or upgrading turbines and equipment for more efficient energy production are all projects that qualify for carbon credits.

Especially lucrative are those projects that curb the emission of methane gas since methane is 21 times more potent than carbon dioxide in terms of contributing to the greenhouse effect.

This is an amazing opportunity for the developing countries to get rich while overhauling their energy infrastructure. It seems to be one case in which you can have your cake and eat it too.

Regional Greenhouse Gas Initiative (RGGI) – The First Three Years

The market-based cap-and-trade system adopted in 2008 (and officially launched on January 1, 2009) by ten Northeastern and Mid-Atlantic states in the United States to reduce emissions of carbon dioxide (CO_2) from power plants. The ten states are Vermont, Rhode Island, Delaware, Maine, New Hampshire, Connecticut, New Jersey, Massachusetts, Maryland, and New York.

As of November 2011, New Jersey was considering to pull out of RGGI.

RGGI has the distinction of being the first mandatory CO_2 cap-and-trade scheme in the United States.

The "carbon allowances" sold to power companies by auction went for at least $1.86 per ton of CO_2 emitted. A total of 12 million allowances (one per ton) went up on the auction block first back in September 2008 by six states. Four more states joined later on. There are more than 200 power plants in the ten-state area and the goal is to reduce total greenhouse-gas emissions by 10% in 2019 (or by 2018, according to some other accounts).

A November 15, 2011 report by Analysis Group documents the positive results of the first three years of RGGI (http://www.analysisgroup.com/uploadedFiles/Publishing/Articles/Economic_Impact_RGGI_Report.pdf).

Here are the highlights from this 50-page report:

•   RGGI is providing positive economic impact (worth a total of $1.6 billion) while meeting emission objectives.

•   The states have used CO2 allowance proceeds creatively – supporting diverse policy and economic outcomes.

•   RGGI has reduced the region's payments for out-of-state fossil fuel by $765 million.

•   RGGI produced new jobs in all ten states to the tune of 16,000 new 'job years' (1 job year=1 year of 1 job).

•   Continue reading on Examiner.com Regional Greenhouse Gas Initiative by the numbers - Providence green policy | Examiner.com http://www.examiner.com/green-policy-in-providence/regional-greenhouse-gas-initiative-by-the-numbers#ixzz1eOqKczYK

•   RGGI helped consumers and businesses alike lower their electricity costs. The average savings were approximately $25 for residential consumers, $181 for commercial consumers, and $2,493 for industrial consumers over the study period (three years).

•   RGGI lowered the revenues of electric power generators by $1.6 billion.

- By 2018, the RGGI states are targeted to reduce their power plant CO2 emissions by 10%.

RGGI states distributed $912 million worth of CO2 allowances through auctions. Here are the amounts generated through such state auctions during the first 3 years:

$52 million for Connecticut , $22 million for Delaware, $27 million for Maine, $170 million for Maryland, $143 million for Massachusetts, $33 million for New Hampshire, $118 million for New Jersey, 327 million for New York, $14 million for Rhode Island, $7 million for Vermont.

Sulfur Dioxide Credits

It's useful to compare the RGGI initiative with the results obtained from a similar market-based scheme to reduce the amount of acid-rain producing sulfur dioxide, a gas released by coal-burning plants and regulated by the U.S. Environmental Protection Agency (EPA).

Thanks to allowing power plants to buy and sell credits to release sulfur dioxide, the presence of this harmful gas in the atmosphere was reduced by 40% since 1992.

Such power companies have installed scrubbers to their smokestacks which reduced the amount of sulfur dioxide released, which in turn allowed them to sell their unused credits at a profit to those companies that did not upgrade their operations with similar pollution-preventing technologies.

COUNTRY FOCUS – Australia

Carbon Tax and Employment

Probably one of the most detailed study of carbon tax's impact on employment has been conducted in Australia and the results are not good for those supporting this policy.

According to the study conducted by the economic consultancy firm ACIL, carbon tax will cost 14,000 jobs in Down Under and decrease exports while targeting to reduce CO_2 emissions by 5% of 2000 levels (or 160 million tons) by 2020.

The main reason would be the dampening effect on Canberra's coal exports to the tune of US $23 billion lost within the first ten years of carbon tax. That loss of revenue translated into 14,000 jobs lost.

Perhaps the result is not surprising given the fact that ACIL study was underwritten by none other than Australian Coal Association (ACA), not exactly an impartial observer of the debate. But still, it reflects the inevitable pressure a coal tax would apply on those high-polluting energy producers who'd rather prefer to do business as usual.

Canberra will levy a carbon tax on the 1,000 top polluting corporations starting July 1, 2012 to the tune of A$23 (£14) for every metric ton of carbon gas produced. The top 500 worst polluters will be charged with a higher tax of AU$23 ($25; £15) for each ton of carbon dioxide they emit.

Deutsche Bank's carbon analyst Tim Jordan said: "This is a very positive step for the global effort on climate change. It shows that the world's most emissions-intensive advanced economy is prepared to use a market mechanism to cut carbon emissions in a low-cost way."

By 2015, Australia plans to shift from carbon tax to a cap-and-trade scheme to regulate emission of greenhouse gases like CO2.

Carbon tax enjoys a limited support among Australia's eminent scientists, medical researchers and environmental activists, including Professor David de Kretser, medical researchers Dr. Fiona Stanley and Sir Gus Nossal, Professor Patrick McGorry, and philanthropist Dame Elisabeth Murdoch.

Australian Prime Minister Julia Gillard is under tremendous pressure from business organizations and especially the mining and coal industry, but she stood her ground. "I take the responsibility for having made that decision. I understand that has caused disappointment among many," she told parliament. "But you get elected to this position to make the tough decisions that are important for the nation's future."

The tax measure is strongly supported (as suspected) by the Greens. "This price on pollution will be seen as an environmental milestone by future generations," said Dr. Jonathan King, a historian and member of the Greens. "They will look back and say: 'Thank God those people in 2011 could see that we were going to suffer if that pollution continued.' It is a turning point in Australian history."

Carbon Tax and Dairy Prices

The new carbon tax will increase the cost of electricity which will in turn cost the dairy farmers of Far North Queensland and extra $10,000 in the first year of implementation, according to James Geraghty, Millaa Millaa dairy farmer and state councilor on the Queensland Dairy Farmers' Organization. Australian Dairy Farmers president Chris Griffin said government help is necessary to help dairy farmers cope with the expected increase in milk production cost due to the carbon tax.

Australia Scraps Carbon Tax (2014 Update)

Australian government has scrapped carbon pricing it established in 2012 with "Clean Energy Act." It's estimated that the CO2 reductions in Australia's National Electricity Market were reduced from 95 megatons annually to 85 megatons within two years between 2012 and 2014.

Prime Minister Tony Abbott, who back in 2009 dismissed global warming as "absolute crap" when he was the opposition leader and attacked the idea of a carbon tax with the slogan "ax the tax" was instrumental in opposing any kind of carbon pricing in Australia.

SOURCE:

https://www.science.org/content/article/australia-scraps-carbon-tax

No Official Carbon Price (2022 Update)

Australia still does not have an official carbon price as would be dictated by a carbon tax. But instead, it has "fuel excise taxes," a politically more palatable form of indirect carbon tax which amounted to EUR 19.23 in 2021 and covers 22.4% of emissions in 2018 as well as in 2021.

SOURCE:

https://www.oecd.org/tax/tax-policy/carbon-pricing-australia.pdf

COUNTRY FOCUS – Brazil

B razil launched serious carbon pricing initiatives back in 2014. The center pillar of these initiatives was not carbon-taxing but a cap-and-trade program.

Twenty companies have participated in a cap-and-trade simulation referred to in the literature as the "EPC-ETS Simulation." These companies were AES Brasil, Anglo American, Banco, Citibank, Banco do Brasil, Itau Unibanco, Braskem, CCR, Construtora Camargo Correa, Duratex S.A, Eletrobras Furnas, Ecofrotas, Grupo Boticario, Klabin, Raizen Energia S.A, Oi S.A, Sanepar, Suzano Papele Celulose, Tam, Telefonica Vivo, and Vale.

The simulation was regarded by ETS observers as Brazil's commitment to leadership in limiting GHGs. The initiative consisted of discussions about "what a robust cap and trade market might entail and how it could be designed and implemented."

Federal Law No. 13576

In 2017, Federal Law No. 13576 has established mandatory GHG emission reduction goals. The mandate was based on a switch from fossil fuels to biofuels.

The law established a certification system for biofuels as well as **decarbonization credits** (issued by biofuel producing companies) that can be traded on stock exchange just like corporate stocks.

In 2018, the simulation — coordinated by Centro de Estudos em Sustentabilidade da Fundação Getulio Vargas (FGVces), was adopted by 29 companies from a wide variety of sectors.

In 2020 Brazil launched new carbon pricing initiatives which considered carbon taxes as well as a pricing instrument.

Sectoral Distribution of Emissions

However, Brazil's industrial sector is responsible for only 2 percent of all GHG emissions while emissions by the energy sector account for 6% of total emissions. Observers argue that a much more effective way to reduce emissions would be to focus on the **Land Use Change (LULUCF) sector** which is the source of a higher percentage of emissions than either the industrial or the energy sector.

However, this sectoral distribution is expected to shift after 2030 with more emphasis on industrial and energy sector developments.

One obstacle to wider adoption of emission-limitation policies is Brazil's determination to become nationally more competitive in the international arena. That's why some Brazilian observers regard carbon pricing schemes as a "threat" to national development targets, which is a sentiment shared by others in countries like India and China as well.

According to OECD, since 2018 only 7.7% of Brazil's emissions from energy use are subjected to carbon pricing. However, the pricing is not a traditional form of a carbon tax. Rather, it's in the

41

form of fuel excise tax which stands at EUR 0.58 as of 2021 – the lowest in G20 countries. In other G20 countries like UK, Italy, and France, for example, the same carbon rate stands between EUR 93 and EUR 96. A huge difference.

Currently the energy sector represents almost 30% of all CO_2 emissions in Brazil with industrial manufacturing, buildings, electric production, agriculture, fisheries, and off-road transportation representing the other 70% of CO_2 emissions.

SOURCES:

https://www.weforum.org/agenda/2014/12/how-brazil-is-testing-carbon-pricing/

https://www.climatescorecard.org/2020/03/brazil-launches-new-private-and-public-policy-carbon-pricing-initiatives/

https://www.oecd.org/tax/tax-policy/carbon-pricing-brazil.pdf

COUNTRY FOCUS –
Canada

C arbon trading in Canada is a market-based mechanism to reduce greenhouse gas emissions. It was introduced in the country by the Kyoto Protocol, which was ratified by the Canadian government in 2002.

The system of carbon trading in Canada has been around for more than 10 years, but it has never been as popular as it is now. This is because the price of carbon credits has fallen due to economic recession, which means that companies are less inclined to purchase them.

A Local Approach to Carbon Pricing

The situation in Canada, which does not have a cap-and-trade system, varies from one region to another. Each province or territory can adopt its own carbon pricing system or can choose the federal piecing system that comes with minimum federal benchmarks.

The federal system has two components:

1.   Fuel Charge – a regulatory tax on fossil fuels (gasoline, natural gas, etc.)

2.   Output-Based Pricing System for different industries

As of 2022, carbon tax is applied in these Canadian territories:

- Northwest Territories
- British Columbia
- Newfoundland and Labrador

Cap-and-Trade is adopted by:

- Quebec
- Nova Scotia

Oil Sands in Alberta

The biggest bone of contention is the 114 billion barrels of oil deposits that reside in the sands of Alberta — the third-largest proven oil reserve in the world. New towns started to emerge in Western Canada overnight to accommodate the new labor force required to produce the "sand oil."

The Political Quilt

Canadian government, instead of a nation-wide cap-and-trade regime, opted to give local states the right to pass CO2 emission permits by industry. Cap-and-trade has been included in the electoral planks of parties like the Liberals, NDP and Bloc Québécois but nothing came out of it since 2008.

British Columbia on the Pacific coast has been the most receptive among the Canadian provinces to the cap-and-trade idea. It joined the Western Climate Initiative (WCI) with seven USA states, including California, and four Canadian provinces. WCI aims to have a working cap-and-trade system in 2012.

Alberta, despite the fact that it's on the verge of becoming an important energy producer state, is closest among the Canadian provinces to a cap-and-trade system.

Intensity Targets

Under an implementation that's been referred to as the "intensity targets" imposed on all industrial emissions, companies operating in Alberta must reduce by 12% a year the amount of energy they use to produce a product. This system also allows the companies to trade emission credits among themselves while trying to hit the annual 12% target.

Carbon Tax

In addition, two Canadian provinces opted for "carbon tax" to limit greenhouse-gas emissions and providing funding for clean alternative-energy projects.

Quebec, Canada adopted carbon tax in October 2007 and charged $3.20 (C$3.50) per metric ton of CO_2. However, cap-and-trade is applied in Quebec as well (2022).

British Columbia similarly adopted in July 2008 a carbon tax to the tune of $9.55 (C$10) per metric ton CO_2 which went up to $4.77 (C$5) per metric ton CO_2 annually until capping at $28.64 (C$30) per metric ton of CO_2 in 2012.

Canada Opposes Kyoto Extension; Comes Under Fire at Durban Conference

Canada officially announced at the Durban Conference on Climate Change on December 5, 2011 that it won't sign up to extend the Kyoto Agreement for another four years after 2012. Instead, it would support another agreement to "eclipse" Kyoto, said Peter Kent, Canada's federal environment minister. South Korean former Prime Minister Han Seung-soo has also gone on record in Durban voicing the same sentiment that the world needs an "alternative system" to the Kyoto Treaty. Japan and Russia also refuse to extend Kyoto while the USA has not even ratified it in the first place.

Peter Kent's remarks drew the ire of not only other countries like South Africa, home to the Durban Conference, but some of his colleagues in the Canadian Parliament as well like NDP's Megan Leslie and Green Party Leader Elizabeth May.

Kyoto Agreement has been signed by 191 countries but is binding on 37 industrial countries only. The United States has not ratified the Kyoto agreement which mandates lowering greenhouse gas emission 6% off 1990 levels. Marching off to its own national tune, Canada aims to lower her emissions by 17% of 2005 levels by 2020.

Even though the Ottawa Government would sign the Kyoto extension, "we will not obstruct those who want to take a second commitment of Kyoto," Kent said at a news conference in Montreal. "Those who wish to continue with Kyoto can continue with a second commitment to Kyoto. We are going to argue in favor of a new agreement, which will eclipse Kyoto."

Canada's position was questioned by South African officials who questioned why Canada participated in the Durban conference if she was not going to support the extension of Kyoto Agreement.

South African Archbishop Desmond Tutu, a widely respected cleric who received Nobel Peace Prize in 1984, led those voices critical of Canada's position.

"Canada, you were once considered a leader on global issues like human rights and environmental protection. Today, you're home to polluting tar sands oil, speeding the dangerous effects of climate change," said a letter, signed by Tutu, a half-dozen South African activists and African environmental groups.

Canada, just like the United States, insist on having major polluters like China, India and Brazil commit themselves to a Kyoto-like regime before they commit themselves officially.

$6.7 billion saving for Canada

By pulling out of Kyoto, Canada would in fact be saving a whopping $6.7 billion in carbon credit payments, according to some analyst.

Canada's greenhouse-gas emissions are 30% higher than the 1990 levels even though it has a 6 percent CO2 reduction target for the end of 2012, according to Kyoto.

According to the Kyoto Treaty, Canada must buy $6.7 billion worth of carbon credits to offset its above-limit-pollution. That represents 890 million tons of CO2 emission above the Kyoto limits at November 2011 prices of about $7.55 a ton. But by declining to be a part of Kyoto extension, Canada would be off the hook and keep her money in her pocket, some analysts argue. Canada is projected to run a C$75.9 billion ($74.8 billion) cumulative budget deficit through the fiscal year ending March 2015.

Timeline of important developments in Canada

2003 — Alberta passed the Climate Change and Emissions Management Act, signaling its commitment to managing greenhouse gas emissions.

March 2007 — Alberta passed Specified Gas Emitters Regulation.

June 2007 — Quebec enacted Canada's first carbon tax, which was intended to earn $2 million per year.

December 2008 — During the 2008 Canadian federal election, Stéphane Dion, then-leader of the Liberal Party, advocated an unpopular revenue-neutral carbon tax. Dion's Liberal Party's lost the election with the lowest percentage of the vote in the country's history.

2014 — A group of public policy economists and retired politicians gathered to begin negotiations on what would become

Canada's Ecofiscal Commission. The Commission has emerged as Canada's primary proponent of carbon pricing.

Feb 2015 — If elected, Justin Trudeau has stated that he will introduce carbon pricing.

Dec 2016 — In a report, ten provinces and the federal government of Canada revealed their "executive, mitigation, and adaptation" policies for a clean economy. Carbon pricing was prominently emphasized in the Pan-Canadian Framework on Clean Growth and Climate Change.

2018 — The Canadian Parliament enacted the Greenhouse Gas Pollution Pricing Act (GHGPPA) as Bill C-74. The GHGPPA uses the term "charge" or "price" rather than "taxation." The levy, which will escalate to $50 per ton of CO2 by 2022, will begin at $20 in 2019 and will gradually increase by $10 each year until 2022.

Dec 2018 — The Canadian Chamber of Commerce (CCC), Canada's largest business organization, has approved the federal government's carbon pricing policy, claiming that it provides flexibility and is the most efficient approach to reduce emissions.

Dec 2020 — Canadian Federal government increased carbon pricing by $15 a ton, to go up to $95 by 2025 and $170 by 2030. The government expects 40% cut in emissions by 2030 as a result of such price hikes.

SOURCES:

https://www.canada.ca/en/environment-climate-change/services/climate-change/pricing-pollution-how-it-will-work.html

https://www.canada.ca/en/environment-climate-change/services/climate-change/pricing-pollution-how-it-will-work/putting-price-on-carbon-pollution.html

https://en.wikipedia.org/wiki/Carbon_pricing_in_Canada

https://www.cbc.ca/news/politics/canada-2030-emissions-reduction-plan-1.6401228

COUNTRY FOCUS –
China

C hina's position on carbon trading and emission controls is crucial since it's one of the world's largest countries.

China has established a "dual carbon" national goal of carbon neutrality by 2060 and peak carbon emissions by 2030.

The country's newly built statewide CO2 emissions trading system — a mechanism that uses market forces to accomplish significant CO2 emission reductions – is supporting these lofty goals, which are part of President Xi Jinping's policy vision of "ecological civilization."

China's system is the **Tradable Performance Standard** (TPS). This statewide program, which began in July 2021 and replaced prior regional pilot programs, is expected to reduce China's CO2 emissions by half by 2060. The TPS currently covers only China's energy industry, but once fully implemented, it will cover eight carbon-intensive industries.

China at Durban Conference

China demanded 5 conditions for emission reduction at Durban Conference.

China, a rapidly developing country which together with the USA **emits 40% of all greenhouse gases in the world**, said it might consider to extent the Kyoto Agreement and accept legally-binding emission limits after 2020 – under certain conditions. The announcement made at Durban Conference on Climate Change created waves among the participants since China's reluctance (like that of USA) to accept any self-imposed emission reduction goals is seen as one of the major stumbling blocks to extend Kyoto.

China asked the industrial countries accept new emission cuts to extend Kyoto. This position contrasts with that of the European Union, for example, which insists on ALL countries accept emission reduction goals.

Xie Zhenhua, China's official envoy to the Durban Conference, revealed the five conditions that must be satisfied before Beijing accepts legally-binding emission targets. One of them is a set of new targets for industrialized countries (a category in which China does not include herself). Two other conditions are: China receiving aid on the latest climate and low-carbon technologies.

During an interview at the Durban Conference, South Korean former Prime Minister Han Seung-soo supported the Chinese position.

"What China wants to do is not to have a verification process by international inspectors who come to China and verify whether they have done it," said Han. "No developing country will do that. India won't do it. Brazil won't do it. They will promise that they will reduce CO2 by 20 percent, 30 percent by a certain year and then they will do it by domestic legislation."

Emissions Trading Scheme (ETS) (2022 Update)

China has adopted a national Emissions Trading Scheme (ETS) in January 2021 instead of a direct carbon tax. The European Union (EU) launched a similar ETS system back in 2005. Chinese Ministry of Ecology and Environment (MEE) is in charge of ETS. The actual trading on the Shanghai Environment and Energy Exchange started on July 16, 2021.

One year into its implementation (as of this writing in 2022), ETS received detailed evaluations from Chinese sources like the non-profit China Dialogue as well as U.S. sources like Center for Strategic and International Studies (CSIS).

In its first phase of implementation, ETS required compliance of 2,000 largest companies in the electrical power generation sector responsible for 40% of CO_2 emissions in China (4.5 billion tons)

ETS system does not rely on an absolute cap of CO_2 emissions but on "**emission intensity**." Emissions are based on **allowances** traded on the Shanghai exchange where one allowance represents 1 ton of CO_2.

Emission intensity is a measure of the amount of CO_2 generated per kilowatt-hour of power (electricity), or per unit of output. For example, in 2021, "the carbon intensity of electricity generation in China was 549.29 grams of carbon dioxide per kilowatt-hour (gCO_2/kWh)." **Reuters** has reported that China has cut down its emission intensity by 18.8% within the last five years (2016-2021).

During the first year (2021), the prices of the traded allowances fluctuated between 30 yuan ($4.72) per ton and 59 yuan ($9.27) per ton.

"Transitioning from carbon intensity-based allocation of allowances to an absolute cap on emissions is increasingly recognized as an important step to improve the effectiveness of the ETS," the ETS observer Huw Slater concluded.

<u>CSIS identified the following factors</u> to determine the success of a carbon pricing system: "(1) whether the system has a sound monitoring, reporting, and verification (MRV) capability; (2) how non-compliance is dealt by the regulatory authority; and (3) whether the price of credits is high enough to incentivize producers to reduce their carbon emissions (or improve efficiency)."

Questioning whether China would succeed on all these three dimensions, CSIS quoted a forecast by International Monetary Fund that "the price of carbon credits will need to reach around $50/ton to effectively drive down carbon emissions in China."

CSIS concluded its analysis in a negative tone: "Although the national ETS is a significant step for China, it is only a small step for the world. This program is unlikely to result in a dramatic reduction in carbon emissions in China by either domestic or foreign companies."

SOURCES:

https://www.csis.org/analysis/chinas-new-national-carbon-trading-market-between-promise-and-pessimism

https://chinadialogue.net/en/climate/the-first-year-of-chinas-national-carbon-market-reviewed/

https://chinadialogue.net/en/climate/how-can-chinas-national-carbon-market-contribute-to-reducing-emissions/

COUNTRY FOCUS – European Union (EU)

European Union has adopted in January 2005 the world's most ambitious cap-and-trade program to date, the **Emissions Trading System (ETS)**, which is binding on the 27 EU-member nations. The initiative targets such CO2 generating industries as utility (power) plants, power, steel and cement factories. Starting in 2012, airlines will have to heed the ETS mandate as well (even though the issue is met by fierce resistance in the USA and China since it will impose extra fees on all flights to and from EU. See the related Issue Focus in this report).

3 Phases

The **first** phase of ETS ran from **2005 to 2008**. The **second** phase (currently underway) will run from **2008 to 2013**. The **third** phase will start in **2013** and end in **2020**. It will expand the ETS's mandate by targeting previously-unregulated industries like ammonia and aluminum manufacturing plants.

The final target of phase three is to reduce CO2 emissions by 21% of 2005 level.

The first phase is considered a FAILURE since it ended with generating a lot more carbon trading permits than the CO2 generated by the polluting companies. A Bloomberg market survey estimated the oversupply at 2.3 percent.

Just as one would expect in a classic supply-and-demand situation, the oversupply of permits reduced the price of carbon pollution since anyone could buy any kind of carbon emission credit for almost nothing and keep on polluting. *Energy Efficiency News* magazine estimated the 2010 price of carbon in UK to be around $20 (E 15) per ton. *EEN* said the price needs to go up to $137 (E 100) per ton to encourage investment in clean alternative energy.

Another implementation that drew criticism during the first phase was the free allocation of carbon permits. Those companies that stayed within their allotted carbon limits, sold the free permits and bagged huge profits.

To prevent the same thing happening again during the second phase of ETS, the European Commission (the executive organ of EU), has increased the amount of reduction on CO2 levels to 5% of 2005 levels, which corresponds to 2 billion tons of carbon dioxide every year.

The SANDBAG Report

A 2010 report by the UK non-profit SANDBAG shows why ETS has not been successful and what to do about it to remedy the situation.

See http://www.sandbag.org.uk/site_media/pdfs/reports/Rescuing_EU_ETS.pdf

Here are some of the highlights of this comprehensive report:

(1)   Inappropriate targets:
ETS targets reducing greenhouse gas emissions in 2020 by 20% of 1990 levels. However, the economic recession of 2009 has already reduced

emissions by 11.6%. Thus the targeted 20% reduction will not represent a true net reduction in emissions, attributable to new measures. Sandbag proposes 30% as a more ambitious but realistic reduction target that would save 1.4 billion tons of CO2.

(2)   Sectoral Overallocation

ETS, currently in its second phase, has 233 million extra allowances, creating a glut of carbon permits in the market. Such oversupply of allowances accumulated during the recession of 2008-2009 will only ensure higher emissions in the future. Therefore Sandbag recommends establishing Phase III caps not on the basis of Phase II allocations but historic emission levels.

(3)   Strategic Carbon Reserve

Sandbag also recommends establishing a "strategic carbon reserve" to hold back a certain number of permits in case the demand for permits drops suddenly, as was the case during 2008-2009 recession. By a controlled release of permits from the strategic reserve, the system can prevent an excessive surplus in permits – as is the case right now (in 2011).

(4)   Unused allocations from earlier phases and those reserved for the New Entrants

About 1.5 billion unused credits will be carried over to Phase III from Phase I, Phase II (830 million), plus those allocated for the New Entrants. The growth in permits should continue until 2017. To prevent the situation get out of hand, "Sandbag recommends an EU wide agreement to control the quantity and quality of offsets, this is to prevent offsets entering the EU which have originated from projects with no or limited sustainable development benefits for the host country."

SOURCES:

https://ember-climate.org/data/data-tools/carbon-price-viewer/

https://carbonmarketwatch.org/our-work/carbon-pricing/eu-carbon-market/

https://climate.ec.europa.eu/eu-action/eu-emissions-trading-system-eu-ets_en

COUNTRY FOCUS – Japan

Japan is a country with a nation-wide **carbon tax**, i.e., the **Global Warming Countermeasure Tax**.

There are also two regional carbon pricing schemes in Japan, **Tokyo ETS** (Emission Trading Scheme) and **Saitama ETS.**

When it comes to cap-and-trade programs in Japan, one needs to look no further than the megacity of Tokyo. With a population of 34 million, Tokyo municipality is like a small country on its own. According to some observers, Tokyo consumes as much energy as the entire Northern Europe. In terms on GNP, the city of Tokyo is cited within the first 20 "largest economies" in the world. It generates a lot of energy, and with it, a lot of greenhouse gases as well.

In April 2010 Tokyo launched Asia's first cap-and-trade program to control CO2 emissions, aiming to reduce the megacity's carbon emissions in 2020 by 25% from 2000 levels.

The first phase of the initiative mandates 1,400 of Tokyo's carbon-emitting companies to cut down their carbon emissions by 6% until 2014. Starting in 2011, those companies that cannot abide by their carbon allowances will be required to purchase additional carbon credits or invest in renewable energy certificates.

The effort to expand the Tokyo cap-and-trade initiative into a nation-wide program met with resistance in the Japanese Parliament and did not lead anywhere at this time of writing.

ETS too modest?

Japanese authors Satoshi Kojima and Kenji Asakawa said even though Japanese ETS platforms were a good start, "the current carbon pricing schemes in Japan are too modest to realize decarbonization transition."

The Case of Japanese Shipping Industry (2022 Update)

Japan boasts the second largest (after Greece) shipping fleet in the world.

The shipping industry is responsible for 3% of greenhouse gas emissions worldwide but it is estimated that it can reach 20% of all emissions by 2050. Marshall and Solomon Islands has already proposed a stiff carbon shipping tax of $100 per ton of CO_2 in 2021.

Japan offered a similar but much more affordable carbon shipping tax of $56 per ton of CO_2 starting in 2025. But, with regular annual increases, the same tax can reach $637 per ton by 2040. Bunker ships would pay three times as much carbon tax since bunker diesel fuel is cheap but very dirty, producing three tons of CO_2 per ton of bunker. It produces 3,500 times more sulfur than the diesel fuel that we put in our cars and trucks.

The amount of taxes collected by Japan will reportedly be used to subsidize zero-emission ships.

Given Japan's weight in international shipping industry (second largest in the world), this proposal will impact other countries and their policy proposals as well. EU, for example, is planning to adopt a similar carbon tax on shipping emissions by 2023 as a part of the "Fit for 55" reform package. This may of course force the shipping companies to look for hubs outside EU in order to lower their costs.

Against the promise of developing zero-emission ships, there are the facts of supply-chain disruptions and rising costs spurred by the COVID pandemic and the Russian invasion of Ukraine. Thus, such proposed benefits of carbon shipping taxes must be weighed against other political and economic factors facing the shipping industry and consumers alike.

SOURCE:

Carbon Pricing in Japan, https://link.springer.com/book/ 10.1007/978-981-15-6964-7

https://news.bloombergtax.com/daily-tax-report-international/carbon-taxes-in-the-shipping-industry-assessing-japans-proposal

COUNTRY FOCUS –
Mexico

Mexico relies primarily on carbon tax for its carbon pricing. Mexico was the first country in the developing world to adopt carbon tax back in 2013. Carbon taxes cover 58% of CO_2 emissions in Mexico.

In 2015 President Enrique Peña Nieto said "Mexico regards carbon pricing is an effective means of reducing greenhouse gas emissions and promoting the use of cleaner fuels."

Mexico's **Intended Nationally Determined Contribution (INDC)** (adopted according to Paris Agreement) aims at reducing greenhouse gas emissions by 22% per cent (of their year 2000 levels) by 2030 and carbon black emissions by 51% per cent by 2050.

Carbon tax, in the form of fuel excise tax, was EUR 25.07 per ton of CO_2 in 2021, down EUR 4.57 when compared to 2018 prices.

As of 2020, the carbon tax was US$ 3.50 (or MXN$ 39.80) per ton of CO_2. Mexican government enjoyed carbon tax revenues of US$ 950,000 million during 2014-15.

Some exceptions to carbon tax include natural gas, jet fuels, and fuel used for manufacturing.

Mexico's leadership in adopting carbon tax confounded observers for three reasons:

1.   Oil production through nationally owned oil giant PEMEX and oil exports are the main source of income for Mexico.
2.   Mexico is not known for her sensitivity to environmental issues. Environmental policy has traditionally not been a main concern in Mexican politics and governance.
3.   Mexico is ruled by a "majoritarian political system and decentralized policy-making" which is not an ideal backdrop for carbon pricing.

Thus Mexico's unpredicted adoption of carbon tax has led scholars to search for new models of casual relationships between political structure and carbon pricing.

In 2018, Mexico launched an ETS Simulation (also known as CarbonSIM Program) with participation of over 100 Mexican corporations from all sectors. The simulation involves a "virtual installation" in a carbon emissions exchange and then the companies are asked to manage their carbon emissions to meet regulatory targets.

3 Steps for Carbon Pricing

Mexico took three steps when developing her carbon pricing policies.

1.   The Mexican Congress passed a law which levied a carbon tax of $3.50 per ton of CO_2 released. Natural gas was exempted to make the tax more politically palatable. The tax was projected to decrease GHG emissions by 1.6 million tons a year and create an extra revenue of $1 billion per year for the government.
2.   Mexico launched a new exchange, MEXICO2, to provide carbon credits to companies with decreased emission levels and encourage decreasing environmental pollution. "These credits can be used to offset costs from the carbon tax," according to World Resources Institute.

3.   In November 2016, Mexico announced her Carbon Market Exercise at COP22 (see Appendix E). This provided a simulation of carbon credit trading, providing data to the government for real carbon trading. Fifty companies participated in this simulation exercise, representing 13 sectors of industry, including the oil and electricity producing giants PEMEX and CFE.

A World Resources Institute study claimed that if the Mexican carbon tax is set at $15 per ton of CO_2 released, that can reduce the GHG emissions by 12 percent.

Highlights of Carbon Pricing Chronology in Mexico

2008 – MOU (Memorandum of Understanding) signed with 6 border states and California to develop protocols to reduce GHG emissions.

2016 – The first forest project and 33 livestock projects.

2017 – First forest credits are issued.

2018 – First landfill credits issued. First urban forest credits issued.

2020 – First aggregate issued credits. First mangrove projects.

2022 – Livestock project. MFP is updated.

SOURCES:

https://www.oecd.org/tax/tax-policy/carbon-pricing-mexico.pdf

https://www.wri.org/insights/mexicos-3-big-steps-towards-comprehensive-carbon-pricing

https://www.climatescorecard.org/2020/03/mexicos-well-established-carbon-tax-and-pilot-emissions-trading-system-with-california-and-quebec/

https://www.gob.mx/epn/en/articulos/mexico-supports-carbon-pricing-initiative?tab=

https://www.tandfonline.com/doi/full/10.1080/09640568.2022.2081136

https://www.nacwconference.com/wp-content/uploads/2022/05/Reserve-Mexico-Program-NACW-2022.pdf

COUNTRY FOCUS – New Zealand

"Deforestation Tax" Controversy

Using "carbon credits" as a tool and an incentive to slow down global warming by rewarding those that release less carbon dioxide to the atmosphere is a policy idea that must be supported by correct policy measures to go along with it. If implemented within a framework of incorrect politics, it can backfire and either handicap the economy with unnecessary restriction and land use patterns or create serious political factions within a country, or both.

A case in point is the "deforestation tax" controversy raging in New Zealand.

It all started when the forest owners in New Zealand felt compelled by market forces to shift their land use from forestry to dairy farming. This would have required cutting down forests to make way for the dairy farms. By 2012, a total of 44,000 hectares of forest are expected to give way to pastures and other uses.

However, there is a problem. When live trees are cut, they eventually release all the carbon dioxide that they have stored inside. Thus, deforestation by definition increases the "carbon footprint" and contributes to the greenhouse effect.

The overall cost of "deforestation liability" is estimated to hit $650 million by 2012 in New Zealand.

As an incentive to stop or slow down the conversion of forests to pastures, the government announced a deforestation tax for trees that were planted before 1990.

But since the tax would be applied only after a certain future date, the decision actually helped accelerate deforestation instead of slowing it down since everybody wanted to beat the deadline and shift to dairy farming without incurring any taxes.

How much such permits should cost? What should be the size limits on forest plots that would be exempted from such a tax? Which year should be declared as the cut-off date for the taxes?

These are all questions with different sets of "winners" and "losers." Unless the political balance between such groups is addressed well, not only social justice but even a country's economic development might be effected adversely while trying to curb greenhouse gases and global warming.

Carbon Farming (2022 update)

Despite the above emphasis on "deforestation," a new sector has emerged in New Zealand in a typical case of "unintended consequences": carbon farming.

This is purchasing large swaths of forests and keeping the trees intact for the purpose of using the trees not for timber but for sucking greenhouse gases from the air. In NZ the number one such gas is not CO2 but Methane due to farm animals.

In NZ, a corporation can offset its carbon emission up to 100% through permits purchased from carbon farmers.

Let's give a concrete example of carbon farming and what this means for the farmers and landowners in New Zealand.

John Hindrup, a farmer from Horehore Station NZ, has bought his land in 2013 "1.8 million New Zealand dollars, sold it this year (2022) for 13 million, or $8.2 million." A profit of over 600% in 9 years.

That kind of profit quickly becomes an undeniable incentive to change land use patterns almost overnight. In 2017, 10,000 acres were converted from pasture to carbon farming. Two years later, the acreage jumped to 90,000 acres: an increase of 9 folds in two short years.

It is estimated that sheep and cattle raising earns 160 NZ dollars per acre annually. Carbon farming is expected to earn 1,000 NZ dollars per acre per year.

Carbon farming seems to be a key component in New Zealand's ambitious goal of becoming "**carbon neutral**" by 2050.

Becoming "carbon neutral" is defined by the NZ government as:

• reducing net emissions of all greenhouse gases (except biogenic methane) to zero by 2050, and
• reducing emissions of biogenic methane to 24–47 per cent below 2017 levels by 2050, including to 10 per cent below 2017 levels by 2030. Since NZ has a robust cap-and-trade or "emission trading" program, such carbon farmers benefit from selling their surplus carbon credits to the carbon-dirty industries.

The Second Unintended Consequence

The unintended consequences of carbon-reduction policies do not end with carbon farming.

When farmland is converted into a forest, the sheep and cattle suffer since they lose their grazing pastures. Given the fact that sheep, cattle, and their off products like wool and steak are NZ's prime exports (15% of total exports), the more farmland is converted to carbon farming, the more traditional NZ exports suffer.

SOURCES:

https://www.nytimes.com/2022/08/11/business/new-zealand-carbon-farming.html

https://environment.govt.nz/acts-and-regulations/acts/climate-change-response-amendment-act-2019/

https://beeflambnz.com/news-views/new-report-confirms-trend-land-use-change

COUNTRY FOCUS – UAE (United Arab Emirates)

The OPEC-member UAE is a **federation of seven emirates**: Abu Dhabi, Ajman, Dubai, Fujairah, Ras al-Khaimah, Sharjah, and Umm al-Quwain. The capital is Abu Dhabi. One of the key officials in the issue of cap-and-trade is Rashid Ahmed bin Fahad, the UAE Minister of Environment and Water.

UAE tries to walk the thin line between those who oppose and favor the continuation of the Kyoto Protocol (limiting the global temperature increase to 2°C). Its **dilemma** is clear for all to see: while being the world's fourth largest oil exporter, UAE also owns MASDAR, the Abu Dhabi company that invests billions all over the world to develop clean alternative energy sources -- which would of course undercut global oil consumption and thus take a chunk out of UAE's oil export revenues.

The more general dilemma shared by all OPEC countries in different degrees is this: every attempt to limit the emission of greenhouse gases like CO2 also results in reduced oil export revenues and GDP for the oil-exporting countries, UAE included. According to an OPEC study, the combined GDP of OPEC countries would fall by a whopping 40% by 2050 if the target of 450 parts per million (ppm) target for CO2 in the atmosphere is adopted.

The middle-of-the-road strategy UAE has opted for is generally referred to as the **"nationally appropriate mitigation actions"** which amounts to individual nations voluntarily adopting their own emission-reduction targets and alternative energy policies. Such a strategy of course would represent a shift from the Kyoto-era practice of poor and less-polluting countries selling carbon credits to richer polluters.

UAE's "nationally appropriate mitigation actions" strategy presents a dilemma for developing nations as well since it would mean the end of the United Nation's the **Clean Development Mechanism (CDM)** which allowed the less-polluting poorer countries to sell their surplus carbon credits to more-polluting richer countries. That would represent a drop in the GDP of poorer countries as well. The total annual market for trading such carbon credits is estimated to be around US $170 billion (as of December 2011). Ivano Iannelli, the chief executive of the Dubai Carbon Centre of Excellence, claimed that 80% of that market would be "wiped out" if the Kyoto Protocol (and thus the CDM regime) is not extended beyond 2012.

But the prospects for the future of carbon trading is not good as these lines are written in December 2011. The price of carbon credits traded in Europe dropped within the last six months of 2011 from €13.69 (US $18.4) a ton to €5.33 (US $7.1).

UAE to Reach Net-Zero Emissions by 2050 (2022 Update)

In a decision that sounds like an oxymoron, UAE declared that it aims to reach net-zero carbon emissions by the year 2050. For a country whose main income is generated with oil extraction, processing, and exporting, it's a courageous stand to take to say the least. Oil and gas exports form 30% of UAE's GDP.

But it could be a farsighted, realistic, and data-driven decision as well. Consider for example the fact that the world's total oil consumption, which stands at 100 million barrels a day, is projected to fall to 24 million barrels a day by 2050. However, despite such futuristic calculations, UAE is still considering increasing its daily production from 4 million to 5 million barrels within ten years (at this writing in 2022).

"With an investment of over (US$165 billion) in renewable energy, our vision for a clean future is clear," is how Forbes quoted UAE prime minister, Sheikh Mohammed bin Rashid al-Maktoum.

Abu Dhabi Launches Carbon Credit Trading Exchange and Clearing House (2022 Update)

Abu Dhabi Global Market (ADGM) has announced in March 2022 that it will launch the "world's first fully regulated" carbon trading exchange and clearing house.

Carbon credits will be traded just like regular corporate stock, helping investment in carbon reduction platforms.

ADGM will partner with ACX, a global carbon exchange company using blockchain technology, to trade commodities, commodity derivates, and similar financial instruments as well. The exchange will hopefully help raising $50 trillion investment said to be necessary to reach net-zero carbon emission goal by 2050.

SOURCES:

https://carboncredits.com/united-arab-emirates-becomes-the-first-persian-gulf-state-to-aim-for-2050-net-zero/

https://www.forbes.com/sites/thebakersinstitute/2021/10/11/the-carbon-neutral-petro-state-an-oxymoron-the-uae-thinks-not/?sh=38eb66344c17

https://www.thenationalnews.com/business/markets/2022/03/29/abu-dhabi-to-launch-worlds-first-carbon-credit-trading-exchange-and-clearing-house/

ISSUE FOCUS - EU to Charge All Airlines for Carbon Emissions

As a part of its Emission Trading System (ETS), the 27-nation European Union (EU)'s plan to start slapping airline companies with "carbon credit buying requirement" is met with stiff resistance by China and USA. ETS is already in enforcement for the emissions of 11,000 plants and factories across the EU.

According to the scheme which went into effect on Jan 1, 2012, all passenger airplanes flying in and out of the 27-nation EU bloc will have to purchase "carbon credits" for emissions above quotas – which comes to 15% of every flight's carbon emissions.

Some experts claim that the cost to the airlines of such a measure will not exceed 0.5% of revenues. But others beg to differ.

China stated that such a measure will deal a blow to China's national airlines by forcing them to pay 85 million euros, or $123 million a year. As a response, threatened to cancel Airbus orders from EU. Moreover, a report from the Chinese Academy of Social Sciences and the China Meteorological Association questioned the basic EU premise and said the measure would not curb emissions.

Twenty countries, China included, has succeeded in getting 36-member International Civil Aviation Organization (ICAO) passing a resolution opposing the inclusion of foreign airlines in the EU plan. The resolution said the EU scheme violated "the cardinal principle of state sovereignty" outlined in the Convention on International Civil Aviation. Japan, Russia, United States, and China are all ICAO members.

The United States, saying that the EU measure tantamount to an interference with international travel, has been equally vociferous in its opposition to the EU move. Air Transport Association of America and the US carriers American Airlines and United Airlines have applied to the European Court of Justice to stop implementation.

Complication

The situation is complicated by the fact that sometimes an airplane flying into Europe burn more fuel outside EU than inside. A flight from San Francisco to London, for example, emits less than 9 percent of carbon in EU territory but 25 percent over the Atlantic, 37 percent over Canada and 29 percent over the United States. Thus paying EU for carbon emissions on such a flight is tantamount to paying EU for carbon emissions that occur 91% over non-EU territory.

Developments in Germany

The reverberations of the EU decision are already felt strongly in German aviation sector. German airlines LUFTHANSA has announced in January 2012 that the measure will add 130 million euros ($168 million) to its 2012 operating budget and hence they need to increase the ticket prices.

Germany's Emissions Trading Authority has allocated 3 billion euros of free carbon permits (corresponding to 42.8 million free permits) until 2020 to German airlines. Any emissions not covered by that subsidy need to be paid for by the individual airline companies. Lufthansa is allocated 12.6 million permits, plus another 2 million permits to the Lufthansa Cargo division. Lufthansa estimates it will have to pay for 35% of its certificates due to the growth of the airlines between 2004-2006 which is taken as a base for all emission measurements.

Austrian Airlines, Swiss and Brussels Airlines will benefit from similar carbon credit subsidies allocated by their respective countries.

SOURCE

https://www.reuters.com/markets/commodities/lead-eu-lawmaker-wants-airlines-pay-their-co2-emissions-sooner-2022-01-20/

DURBAN SUMMIT

United Nations Climate Change Conference, a.k.a. "Durban Summit," was held in Durban, South Africa, November 28 - December 9, 2011, with the participation of 192 countries.

The summit is also referred to as "COP17/CMP7" since it's the 17th Conference of the Parties (COP17) to the United Nations Framework Convention on Climate Change (UNFCCC) and the 7th Session of the Conference of the Parties serving as the Meeting of the Parties (CMP7) to the Kyoto Protocol, which ends in 2012.

Whether the Kyoto Protocol will be extended and if so how have been the main points of discussion at the Summit.

The rich Western and developing countries (mainly in Asia) have been at odds about the green-gas emission limits imposed in Kyoto. United States, for one, has never signed the protocol arguing that unless big polluters like China and India agree to live by protocol terms it doesn't make any sense to join it. The opposition to the protocol is equally adamant in Japan, Russia and Canada.

In the opening session of the Summit, the EU took a hard stance and expressed its displeasure for not seeing any progress on the part of the developing countries to take domestic measures to limit and reduce their emissions.

"It's very important that other major economies join the effort. It would not make sense for only the EU to take on a second commitment under the Kyoto protocol," said Joanna Mackowiak-Pandera, Poland's under-secretary of state for the environment. Since Poland held the EU presidency in 2011, it also led the EU delegation to the Summit.

EU defended the principle of "legal parallelism" if Kyoto is to be extended beyond 2012; that is, if the EU signs up to an international legally binding treaty, developing countries like India and China should also do likewise.

The EU has the most ambitious carbon-dioxide-reduction goals in the world, aiming to cut its emissions to 20% of 1990 levels, by 2020. The EU also pledged to increase that to 30% if other countries promised to do likewise.

Brazil and South Africa side with India and China on the issue of voluntary emission reductions since all of them (just like Poland) use cheap (and dirty) coal to fire up their utility plants — a crucial ingredient for generating all the electricity that these nations need to continue their industrialization efforts.

Canada was singled out early in the Summit for violating the spirit and letter of the Kyoto Protocol for going ahead with projects to produce oil from tar sands of Alberta. A pipeline is in the works to carry the oil from Canada through USA down to the Gulf of Mexico. 114 billion barrels of oil was discovered in the oil-sands of Alberta, Canada; the third-largest proven oil reserve in the world. Canada does not have a cap-and-trade system to reduce CO2 pollution.

Among the hot topics of discussion at the Summit was the establishment of a $100 billion fund to help the poorer countries cope with the requirements of climate change. 16 aid and environmental groups wrote a letter to the U.S. Secretary of State Hillary Clinton, accusing the United States of blocking progress on the formation of the fund.

Even though he was elected with the full support of environmental groups back in 2008, President Obama is regarded as falling behind in his promises. "Three years later, America risks being viewed not as a global leader on climate change, but as a major obstacle to progress," the letter says. "US positions on two major issues – the mandate for future negotiations and climate finance – threaten to impede in Durban the global co-operation so desperately needed to address the threat of climate change."

Climate Ethics Campaign (CEC) joined others in claiming that the United States had a "moral obligation" to reduce greenhouse gas emissions as an industrialized nation that also holds the dubious distinction to be the world's worst greenhouse-gas emitter in history.

The Result – Good or Bad?

The Durban Summit ended with the participants signing the Durban Platform for Enhanced Action to extent the Kyoto Protocol by another five years and commit all major polluters to a legal obligation to reduce their emissions by 2020. The signers agreed to "develop a new protocol, another legal instrument or agreed outcome with legal force." The discussions for the "new protocol" will start in 2015.

Also agreed was the founding of a "Green Climate Fund" to help the poorer countries finance the efforts to reduce their greenhouse gas emissions.

The result was hailed as positive by those like the President of the Maldives, Mohamed Nasheed. Most of 1190 islands that make up of the

Maldives is threatened by floods and submersion if the water levels continue to rise as a result of global warming.

South African Foreign Minister Maite Nkoana-Mashabane who chaired the summit was equally upbeat: "We have made history," he said.

Others like Friends of the Earth executive director Andy Atkins claimed that the summit ended with an "empty shell of a plan" since none of the major polluters would be forced to do anything about the current situation until 2020. Giving credence to such a claim was the insistence of the United States on "voluntary reductions" instead of a legally binding agreement.

Another split was between politicians, diplomats, investors and entrepreneurs, on the one hand, and NGOs and environmental groups, on the other. The former group liked the Durban results while the latter slammed it .

The critics point out that the summit agreement to "develop a new protocol, another legal instrument or agreed outcome with legal force" is so vague and flexible it really means nothing at all since every country can interpret it in any way they like.

German daily media, for one, criticized the results almost unanimously. Here are some excerpts:

Die Tageszeitung (left of center): "The losers are the small and vulnerable countries that are hit especially hard by climate change."

Frankfurter Allgemeine Zeitung (center right): "The results of the Durban conference were meager. It has kept the sluggish process of negotiations alive -- but that's about it."

Frankfurter Rundschau (center left): "[The Durban Summit is] almost useless. The UN summit wasn't a debacle like the Copenhagen conference two years ago, but it only narrowly avoided complete failure -- like most of the 16 summits before it."

Süddeutsche Zeitung (center left): "Durban hasn't solved any problems, it has merely offered the prospect of a solution."

Handelsblatt (investment and business): "Durban has shown once again that global climate conferences aren't a suitable forum for effective climate protection."

SOURCE

https://unfccc.int/process/conferences/the-big-picture/milestones/outcomes-of-the-durban-conference

ARGUMENT: Why Stop at Carbon Credits?

Some of the proposed solutions for global warming like capping-and-trading of carbon credits can actually be transferred to other sectors and applied to other pressing social problems as well.

Take education in general, and the quest for eliminating illiteracy in particular, for example.

Why not create an artificial scarcity of illiteracy just like creating an artificial scarcity of carbon dioxide emissions?

Just like both the private sector and the Congress are working in parallel tracks to determine a cap on the kind of "carbon footprint" that private corporations can have without incurring any penalties, the Congress, private sector and the municipalities can also work on an artificial cap on the percentage of illiteracy that will be allowed in a city, county, state, or even corporation.

Different "certificates" or "permits" can be issued for different levels of "illiteracy."

Then, the entities that are below their "illiteracy quotas" can sell their permits to those entities that have too many illiterates. Hopefully the cost of buying such permits will be so prohibitive that the entity in question will soon see the benefit of marshaling all its resources to bring its illiteracy level to within the cap limits.

And what if an entity can neither afford such illiteracy credits nor pull its illiteracy to within the cap limits? You obviously cannot "shut down" a city as though it were a corporation.

Perhaps Congress and state legislators can index such compliance to withholding of various funds from the state or federal budget?

At some point this should have a positive snowballing effect on those who comply fast with such illiteracy caps - not only they would make money by selling their permits but also they would enhance the educational attainment of their workforce even further by channeling such new funds again into their educational system. Thus we have to admit that this idea carries in its nucleus the danger of making the good even better while punishing the already disadvantaged even further - unless they do something about it.

Sometimes such real and credible threats, on the one hand, and real and credible rewards, on the other, are exactly what is needed to galvanize whole communities into serious action and give them the necessary motivation to achieve what has until then been deemed "impossible."

GLOSSARY

Assigned Amount

Emission quotas assigned by the Kyoto Protocol.

BAU

Business As Usual.

CARB

California's Air Resources Board.

Carbon Dioxide

Fossil fuels like oil, gas, and coal are made up of carbon and hydrogen atoms. When the fuel is burned, the energy in the carbon-hydrogen bonds is released, thus providing warmth and energy. But in that burning process, carbon atoms are released. Each carbon atom unites with two oxygen atoms, forming Carbon Dioxide (CO_2), a greenhouse gas that absorbs and traps heat in the atmosphere. That's why CO_2 is called a "greenhouse gas" since eventually it may turn earth's atmosphere into a gigantic warm and humid greenhouse.

Carbon Leakage

Describes a situation in which greenhouse-gas emissions from one nation state affects another.

Cap

The limit placed on the amount of greenhouse gases a corporation or entity can release into the atmosphere.

CES

Clean Energy Standard.

CDM

Clean Development Mechanism. A part of the Kyoto Protocol. CDM allows companies and governments in industrialized countries to fund programs to reduce emissions in developing countries as an alternative to undertaking similar but more expensive action at home.

CER

Certified Emission Reduction(s).

Chicago Climate Exchange (CCX)

Chicago Climate Exchange (CCX) was set up in 2003 to regulate the buying and selling of "carbon credits". Among the groups that provided seed money for CCX was the Joyce Foundation which boasted as a board member a young Barack Obama, not yet elected President at the time.

CCX was supported by major Fortune 100 corporations like Ford, Bank of America, IBM, Amtrak and Intel, as well as such investment powerhouses as Goldman Sachs, Climate Change Capital and Al Gore's Generation Investment Management. But despite all that support, CCX had to close doors in 2010.

Among the major national organizations that supported CCX were National Farmers Union and the Iowa Farm Bureau and such universities as University of California, San Diego, Tufts University, Michigan State University and University of Minnesota.

One goal of the companies participating in CCX was to reduce their total emissions by 6% by 2010.

At its height, the exchange enjoyed 400 corporate members. It was a well-meaning market experiment in reducing the mission of greenhouse gases that went nowhere.

CO_2

Carbon Dioxide.

CPP

Clean Power Plan.

CTC

Carbon Tax Center. Charles Komanoff and Daniel Rosenblum launched the Carbon Tax Center in January 2007. The main message of the center is: taxing emissions of carbon dioxide — the primary greenhouse gas — is imperative to reduce global warming. http://www.carbontax.org/

EKC

Environmental Kuznets Curve. The theory that as economies develop they generate a lot of pollution but after a certain point the pollution first levels off and then starts to decrease due to better clean-up technology and citizen involvement in anti-pollution measures.

Emissions Trading System (ETS)

The world's most ambitious cap-and-trade program to date adopted by the European Union (EU). ETS is binding on the 27 EU-member nations. For more, please see the related *Country Focus* section of this report.

EPA

(United States) Environmental Protection Agency.

ETC
Emissions Trading System.

EUA

EU Allowance. The carbon credits or pollution permits traded in the EU Emissions Trading Scheme (ETS).

Feed-in-Tariff (FIT)

"Feed-in-Tariff" (FIT), also known as a "standard offer contract," is a government regulation designed to encourage investment in renewable energy systems like solar panels and wind farms. The policy offers long-term energy purchasing contracts at subsidy prices to those business owners who generate alternative energy, including wind and solar. Wind is offered a lower contract price than solar, reflecting the wind power's lower generation cost.

The thinking behind this policy is to support renewals energy investors by providing a long-term price and revenue stability.

Conservative critics state that FIT ends up raising utility bills and thus hurts the average consumer instead of helping them. The result, the critics claim, while the well-off investors get richer the utility consumers get poorer, thus widening the existing income gap between the haves and the have-nots.

GHG

See: Greenhouse Gases

Greenhouse Gases

Greenhouse gases (GG or GGS) like water vapor, carbon dioxide, methane, nitrous oxide, sulfur dioxide, and ozone absorb radiation from heat sources. That's why the more GG in the atmosphere, the warmer the atmosphere gets. Thus follows the attempt to limit GG to fight global warming.

Greenwashing

An attempt by corporations to make their environmental credentials look better than they actually are.

HFCs

Hydrofluorocarbons.

IEA

International Energy Agency.

Intensity Standard

See Tradable Performance Standard.

IPCC

United Nations Intergovernmental Panel on Climate Change.

Kyoto Protocol

An international protocol for clean environment that grew out of the United Nations Framework Convention on Climate Change (UNFCC) held in 1997 in Kyoto, Japan. The Kyoto Protocol was adopted in 2005 without the US ratifying it. The protocol mandates UN countries to reduce their emissions of greenhouse gases by at least 5% below 1990 levels by Jan 1,

2012, its original termination date. However, the protocol was extended by another 5 years beyond 2012 at the U.N. Durban Summit held in December 2011, Durban, South Africa.

Leakage

An unforeseen problem in the implementation of carbon tax, or any other punitive fee, is what's referred to as "leakage".

"Leakage" means a company which is penalized for emitting green-house gases shutting down its doors in one state but continuing production in another so that the emission "savings" in one state is neutralized by increased emissions in another. Due to the rights and different legal structures that states enjoy in the United States, "leakage" emerges as a real obstacle in making "carbon tax" a feasible solution to stop the emission of green-house gas emissions.

Legal Parallelism

The EU principle which demands that if EU signs up for an extension of the Kyoto Protocol, industrializing countries like China and India must sign for the same kind of commitment as well.

MAC

Marginal Abatement Cost. The marginal cost of reducing pollution. As environmental pollution is reduced, MAC goes up since more expensive and sophisticated technologies need to be used to get rid of it.

NDC

See Nationally Determined Contributions.

Nationally Determined Contributions

What 196 countries who signed the Paris Protocol in 2015 agreed to submit to combat climate change.

NOx

Nitrogen Oxide.

Peaker Plant

A power plant that starts generating electricity when electricity demand peaks in the nearby grid.

Rate Based Standard

See Tradable Performance Standard.

Renewables Obligation (RO)

"Renewables Obligation" (RO) is a British policy tool very similar to carbon credits, aimed to encourage the generation of renewal energy. It demands that utility companies generate some portion of their electricity from renewable energy sources.

Companies must present Renewables Obligation Certificates (ROCs) to prove that they are meeting their obligations. Those who cannot, can purchase ROCs from those who produce more that their quote of renewables, thus creating a market for the buying and selling of these certificates. One result of such trade is the higher cost of energy production for those companies who are purchasing ROCs to stay in business. Market forces, the classic mechanism of supply-and-demand, is supposed to eventually regulate the ROC prices and create clean energy at "market prices."

Regional Greenhouse Gas Initiative (RGGI)

Regional Greenhouse Gas Initiative. The cap-and-trade system adopted in 2008 (and officially launched on January 1, 2009) by ten Northeastern and Mid-Atlantic states in the United States to reduce emissions of carbon dioxide (CO_2) from power plants. The ten states are Vermont,

Rhode Island, Delaware, Maine, New Hampshire, Connecticut, New Jersey, Massachusetts, Maryland, and New York.

SO_2

Sulfur Dioxide.

Sustainable Growth

The idea that economies can continue to grow while keeping the environmental damage at a level where the environment can renew its resources.

TPS

See Tradable Performance Standard. Also: Rare-Based Standard, Intensity Standard.

Tradable Performance Standard

A carbon trading and pricing scheme in which not the total amount of emissions but emissions per unit of output are regulated. TPS is the system put into use by China in 2021. TPS encourages low-intensity production of GHG while discouraging those enterprises with high-intensity emissions. In the USA, EPA used TPS to reduce the lead in gasoline.

UNFCCC

United Nations Framework Convention on Climate Change (UNFCC) held in 1997 in Kyoto, Japan. A.K.A. "Kyoto Protocol."

WCI

Western Climate Initiative. The union formed in 2007 by seven USA states, including California, and four Canadian provinces to have a cap-and-trade system in operation in 2012.

WMO

World Meteorological Organization

NOTES

NOTES

APPENDIX A: Selected Recent Developments

(Listed chronologically, from the most recent to oldest news item.)

Bloomberg Supports BeyondCoal.org with $50 Mil

BeyondCoal.org is a coalition of anti-coal groups that succeeded stopping the construction of 160 coal-powered power plants within the last 10 years. New York Mayor Michael Bloomberg's foundation donated $50 million to BeyondCoal.org to support the drive for clean energy. Here is a map of coal-fired plants that will NOT be built, thanks to the campaign of organizations like BeyondCoal.org: http://www.vancouverobserver.com/sites/vancouverobserver.com/files/resize/images/blog/body/beyond-coal-150_0-500x292.jpg

Durban Summit

United Nations Climate Change Conference, a.k.a. "Durban Summit," was held in Durban, South Africa, November 28 - December 9, 2011, with the participation of 192 countries.

6 U.S. States Abandon WCI

Six U.S. States — New Mexico, Arizona, Washington, Oregon, Montana and Utah — pull out of WCI (Western Carbon Initiative) on November 18, 2011. That leaves California and four Canadian provinces still members of WCI.

California Adopts Cap-and-Trade

An important development of 2011 is the State of California becoming the first U.S. state to adopt an official cap-and-trade program in October 2011. During the first phase beginning in 2013, the state's carbon producers will be forced either to stay within the pollution limits mandated by this regulation or purchase carbon credits. The companies that emit more than 25,000 tons of carbon dioxide a year must get a permit to do so. The second phase will be launched in 2015 and cover 85% of the carbon-emitting organizations in California. (See *"10 Questions About California's Cap-and-Trade Program"* http://switchboard.nrdc.org/blogs/kgrenfell/10_questions_about_californias.html)

Australia Adopts Carbon Tax, to start June 2012

Australia will levy a carbon tax on the 1,000 top polluting corporations starting July 1, 2012 to the tune of A$23 (£14) for every metric ton of carbon gas produced. The top 500 worst polluters will be charged with a higher tax of AU$23 ($25; £15) for each ton of carbon dioxide they emit.

Oil-Sands of Alberta, Canada

114 billion barrels of oil was discovered in the oil-sands of Alberta, Canada. That's the third largest proven oil reserve in the world, following those of Saudi Arabia (264 billion) and Venezuela (211 billion barrels. Such a new reserve of oil that will soon be pumped into the USA and world markets is expected to lessen the enthusiasm for adopting new cap-and-trader programs. (For more, see: http://www.bloomberg.com/news/2011-11-22/oil-abundance-in-canada-sands-provoking-anxiety-over-lust-for-fossil-fuels.html)

EU to Charge All Airlines

The EU plan to charge all airlines flying in and out of EU for carbon emissions created a fierce backlash. Please see the related Issue Focus in this report.

Resistance to Kyoto

On an international level the opposition to Kyoto Treaty (which underlies the whole logic and impetus for the cap-and-trade) is also fading. Russia, Japan and Canada announced at the 2011 G8 meeting that they would soon leave Kyoto. The United States never signed it in the first place, arguing that the treaty presents an undue disadvantage and an unfair obstacle for the economies of developed countries when major polluters like China refuse to cap their carbon emissions.

IEA Warning on Record-Level Global Carbon Emissions

The International Energy Agency (IEA) issued a press release in May 2011 stating that the carbon emissions in 2010 have broken the 2008 record by 5%, with China and India appearing to count for most of the rise, and hit the 30.6 giga-tons mark. Such a record-level rise puts a pressure on all cap-and-trade programs since that means lower carbon emission quotas, higher prices for carbon credits, higher carbon taxes, or a combination of all three.

The IEA's Fatih Birol said the finding was "another wake-up call. The world has edged incredibly close to the level of emissions that should not be reached until 2020 if the 2C [degrees above pre-industrial levels] target is to be attained."

World Bank Alarm

The rate for carbon credits in the international market hovered around 11 to 12 Euros per ton back in March 2007.

In 2011, however, the World Bank issued an alarm about the total volume of trade which amounted to only $1.5bn (£916m) of credits traded in 2010. This is the lowest volume since carbon credits started to be traded back in 2005, the year when Kyoto Protocol to limit greenhouse gas emissions was signed.

Clearly the pace and enthusiasm is ebbing away in the face of economic down turn in the West and political opposition to the idea. The same number was $25bn in 2009. The downward trend is unmistakable at this writing.

NOTES

APPENDIX B: Timeline of Important Milestones

1967 – 1970 -- Ellison Burton and William Sanjour, two scientists working for the U.S. National Air Pollution Control Administration (predecessor to the United States Environmental Protection Agency's Office of Air and Radiation) study the "cap and trade" model to control atmospheric pollutants by running a series of micro-economic computer simulation models.

1972 — West Germany saw more international scientific cooperation on the greenhouse subject as important at the United Nations Conference on the Human Environment, led by Nobel Prize-winning West German Chancellor Willy Brandt and Swedish Prime Minister Olof Palme.

1977 — Sir Crispin Tickell's book Climatic Change and World Affairs is published, deemed essential in starting the process of persuading the British government.

1979 — First World Climate Conference convened in Geneva.

1980 — The greenhouse effect is examined in the energy chapter of the Brandt Report, which was released in New York and discusses unequal North-South growth.

1984 – New York [State] creates the nation's first cap-and-trade program for air pollution.

1985 – Some New England states began to impose air pollution rules.

1990 – U.S. Congress amends the Clean Air Act to create a national program based on New York's model. "Cap and trade" is included in Title IV of the Act.

1991 — The First Global Revolution is published by the Club of Rome. This book argues for a more holistic approach to climate change, including energy production, population expansion, water availability, food production, and other environmental challenges.

1992 – Earth Summit convenes in Rio de Janeiro, Brazil.

1995 – The new Clean Air Act caps on NOx and SO2 gases take effect. According to the Pacific Research Institute, an American think tank, acid rain levels in the U.S. have dropped by 65 per cent since 1976.

1996 — The European Union has set a target of a maximum 2°C increase in world average temperature.

1997 – United Nations Framework Convention on Climate Change (UNFCC) held in Kyoto, Japan. The "Kyoto Protocol," which grew out of this conference, will expire in 2012.

1997 – The State of Illinois in USA adopts the Emissions Reduction Market System, a trading program for credits of over 100 pollutants in of the Chicago area.

2001 — President George W. Bush of the United States officially withdrew from the Kyoto Accords.

2003 – Chicago Climate Exchange (CCX) opens.

2003 – The U.S. Environmental Protection Agency (EPA) launches the NOx Budget Trading Program (NBP), a market-based cap and trade program.

2003 – The New South Wales (NSW) state government in Australia announces the NSW Greenhouse Gas Abatement Scheme.

2005, January – The European Union Emission Trading Scheme (EU ETS) comes into effect to meet the caps set by the Kyoto Protocol.

2005 – The Kyoto Protocol is adopted in 2005 without the US ratifying it.

2006 – The State of California in USA passes the California Global Warming Solutions Act, signed by Governor Arnold Schwarzenegger.

2007, February – Seven U.S. states and four Canadian provinces join hands to create the Western Climate Initiative (WCI),a regional greenhouse gas emissions trading system with the goal to have a cap-and-trade system in place in 2012.

2008, January – Norway, Iceland, and Lichtenstein join the European Union Emission Trading Scheme (EU ETS).

2008 – Ten U.S. States sign up for the Regional Greenhouse Gas Initiative (RGGI).

2008 – U.S. Presidential candidate Barack Obama promises on the campaign trail to focus on cap-and-trade as a way to control the emission of greenhouses gases. He said he would "set a hard cap" on carbon emissions with the goal of reducing them 80 percent by 2050 (ABC News).

2008, September – New Zealand government legislates the New Zealand Emissions Trading Scheme (NZ ETS).

2009, June 26 – The U.S. House of Representatives by a narrow vote of 219-212 passes The American Clean Energy and Security Act (H.R. 2454), a greenhouse gas cap-and-trade bill. It is also known as the **Waxman-Markey Bill**. The bill, however, was not approved by the U.S. Senate. The Bill proposed to reduce American emissions by 3 per cent of 2005 levels by 2012, 17 per cent by 2020, 42 per cent by 2030, and 83 per cent by 2050.

2010 – Chicago Climate Exchange (CCX) closes its doors.

2010, April – Tokyo, Japan kicks off Asia's first cap-and-trade program. According to some observers, Tokyo consumes as much energy as the entire Northern Europe. The first phase mandates 1,400 of Tokyo's carbon-emitting companies to cut down their carbon emissions by 6% until 2014. Starting in 2011, those Tokyo companies that cannot abide by their carbon allowances will be required to purchase additional carbon credits or invest in renewable energy certificates.

2010 – USA government announces it will invest $15 billion per year for the next 10 years to support the development of "clean energy." The funds for this cap-and-trade program will be raised the auction sale of greenhouse gas (GHG) emissions credits to the highest bidder. The program is expected to generate $78.7 billion in additional revenue in FY 2012, increasing to $83 billion by FY 2019.

2011, February – Australian government proposes a Clean Energy Bill.

2011 – New Jersey announces its intention to pull out of RGGI.

2011 – The United States adopts the Cross-State Air Pollution Rule (CSAPR), establishing for trade groups for SO_2 and NOx credits.

2011, October – The State of California becomes the first U.S. state to adopt an official cap-and-trade program. During the first phase beginning in 2013, the state's carbon producers will be forced either to stay within the pollution limits mandated by this regulation or purchase carbon credits. The second phase will be launched in 2015 and cover 85% of the carbon-emitting organizations in California. (See *"10 Questions About California''s Cap-and-Trade Program"* http://switchboard.nrdc.org/blogs/kgrenfell/10_questions_about_californias.html)

2011, November – Six American states (New Mexico, Arizona, Washington, Oregon, Montana and Utah) withdraw from the Western Climate Initiative, leaving only California and four Canadian provinces.

2011, November-December — United Nations Climate Change Conference, a.k.a. "Durban Summit," was held in Durban, South Africa, November 28 - December 9, 2011, with the participation of 192 countries. Canada officially announced at the Durban Conference on Climate Change that it won't sign up to extend the Kyoto Protocol for another four years after 2012. However, the participants agreed to extend the Kyoto Protocol by another 5 years.

2012, June – "Rio+20" Environmental Summit convenes in Rio de Janeiro, Brazil with the participation of 188 countries. The Group of 77 Nations asked the economic burden of environmental cleanup be shouldered by older industrialized nations like EU and the USA rather than developing nations like China and India.

2012, November – In the California cap and trade auction, businesses pay $11.50 a ton for the CO_2 emission permit.

2013, December – Columbia University holds The Earth Summit in NYC.

2013, July – European Parliament by a vote of 344-311 passes a law in support of the cap-and-trade program. The law aims to increase the price of carbon permits which fell to a concerning low due to an oversupply of permits.

2013-2014 – California is criticized for using the Greenhouse Gas Reduction Fund monies to bullet trains, water conservation projects, and $500 million borrowed to balance the state's general fund budget.

2014 – California regulators cap the total annual allowed CO2 emissions at 160 million metric tons (mmt). The number will go up to 395 mmt in 2015, to fall to 334 mmt by 2020. The State of California has sold $2.27 billion of CO2 permits.

September 23, 2014 – U.N. hosts a Climate Summit in New York City, USA. A call was made to the private sector to take the lead on "carbon pricing."

September 22-28, 2014 – New York City observed and celebrated the Climate Week.

December 2015 - The Paris Agreement. World leaders met in Paris for the 21st Conference of the Parties of the UNFCCC. All countries were asked to commit themselves to emission-reduction targets.

August 3, 2015 - President Barack Obama of the United States announces the Clean Power Plan, which aims to cut pollution and greenhouse gas emissions.

April 2017 - Protests against President Donald Trump's climate change policies took place, including the March for Science and the 2017 People's Climate March.

June 2017 - The United States has withdrawn from the Paris Agreement due to President Donald Trump's decision.

October 8, 2018 - The IPCC Special Report on Global Warming of 1.5°C was released, warning catastrophic environmental repercussions if global warming exceeds 1.5°C.

April 28, 2019 - Representatives Alexandria Ocasio-Cortez and Ed Markey of the Democratic Party submitted a resolution in the US House of

Representatives calling for a Green New Deal, which will have limited immediate impact but would be a major campaign issue in the 2020 presidential election.

September 2019 – The UN Secretary-General António Guterres has convened the 2019 UN Climate Action Summit in an attempt to press countries to commit to 45 percent greenhouse gas reductions by 2030 and carbon neutrality by 2050, but the talks have been hampered by the absence of the two largest carbon emitters, China and the United States.

December 1, 2019 – The European Commission publishes a European Green Deal with the goal of achieving climate neutrality in Europe by 2050.

December 2019 – The 25th Conference of Parties comes to a close with no concrete action on climate change policy.

January 2021 – President Joe Biden signs an executive order re-joining the Paris Climate Agreement.

August 7, 2021 – The IPCC's Sixth Assessment Report was released, projecting that current emissions levels will likely result in 1.5°C warming within the next two decades, and calling for immediate action to avoid additional catastrophic warming.

October 31-November 12, 2021 — After being postponed owing to the COVID-19 pandemic, the 26th Conference of the Parties is set to take place in Edinburgh, United Kingdom.

June 2022 — Bonn Climate Change Conference held in Bonn, Germany.

August 29 – September 2, 2022 — Africa Climate Week 2022 was held in Gabon, Africa.

NOTES

APPENDIX C: Support for and Opposition to H.R. 2454

Those who supported American Clean Energy and Security Act (ACES) of 2009 H.R. 2454:

- Obama Administration and most Democrats.

- Sierra Club

- Union of Concerned Scientists

- One Sky

- Clean Water Action

- American Rivers

- Environmental Defense Fund

- Kleiner Perkins et al

- NRG Energy

- Public Service Enterprise Group

- Hewlett Packard

- National Audubon Society

- Pew Environment Group

- Applied Materials

- Nike

- Aspen Snowmass

- Clif Bar and Company

- FPL Group

- OXFAM America

- DuPont

- VoteVets.org

- Alliance for Climate Protection

- Austin Energy

- Symantec Corporation

- Seventh Generation

- World Resources Institute

- Laborers' International Union of North America

- The American Civil Rights Union

- Communications Workers of America

- Utility Workers Union of America

- United Steelworkers

- Alcoa

- Dow Chemical Company

- Boston Scientific Corporation

- Starbucks Corporation

- AES Corporation

- Deere & Company

- Nature Conservancy

- Service Employees International Union

- Exelon Corporation

- Duke Energy Corporation

- National Grid

- Levi Strauss & Co.

- eBay, Inc.

- Avista Corporation

- Natural Resources Defense Council

- Shell

- PG&E Corporation

- Chrysler

- Climate Solutions

- Johnson & Johnson

- General Electric

- League of Conservation Voters

- Ford Motor Company

- Environment America

- PepsiCo

- PNM Resources

- Rio Tinto

- Siemens Corporation

- General Motors

- Alstom Group

Those who opposed American Clean Energy and Security Act (ACES) of 2009 H.R. 2454:

- Most Republicans

- Greenpeace American Farm Bureau Federation

- Friends of the Earth

- Rainforest Action Network

- Public Citizen

- Murray Energy Corporation

- American Petroleum Institute

- American Conservative Union

- American Shareholders Association

- College Republican National Committee

- National Pork Producers Council

- Americans for Tax Reform

- National Taxpayers Union

- National Mining Association

- Alliance for Worker Freedom

- Ethan Allen Institute

- International Rivers

- Dr. James E. Hansen (a strong Global Warming advocate)

Source: http://www.opencongress.org/bill/111-h2454/money

APPENDIX D: Useful Web Sites

Center for Climate and Energy Solution

http://www.pewclimate.org/

EPA, Cap and Trade

http://www.epa.gov/capandtrade/

Wikipedia: Emissions Trading

http://en.wikipedia.org/wiki/Emissions_trading

New York Times: Cap and Trade

http://topics.nytimes.com/topics/reference/timestopics/subjects/g/greenhouse_gas_emissions/cap_and_trade/index.html

Center for American Progress: Cap and Trade 101

http://www.americanprogress.org/issues/2008/01/capandtrade101.html

YouTube: The Story of Cap and Trade

http://www.youtube.com/watch?v=pA6FSy6EKrM

California Air Resources Board: Cap and Trade

http://www.youtube.com/watch?v=pA6FSy6EKrM

NPR: How Cap and Trade Was Trashed

http://www.npr.org/templates/story/story.php?storyId=126280761

Environmental Defense Fund: What is Cap and Trade?

http://www.edf.org/page.cfm?tagID=22819

Beyond Coal

http://www.BeyondCoal.org

APPENDIX E: List of Earth Summits

1972 - The United Nations Conference on the Human Environment (UNCHS) in **Stockholm**, Sweden.

1982 - The 1982 Earth Summit in Nairobi (Kenya). An Earth Summit was held in **Nairobi**, Kenya, from 10 to 18 May 1982.

1992 - The United Nations Conference on Environment and Development (UNCED) or Earth Summit in **Rio de Janeiro** (Brazil).

2002 - The World Summit on Sustainable Development, Earth Summit 2002 or Rio+10, **Johannesburg** (South Africa).

2009 - United Nations Climate Change Conference or Copenhagen Summit, **Copenhagen** (Denmark).

2012 - The United Nations Conference on Sustainable Development (UNCSD) or Rio+20, **Rio de Janeiro** (Brazil).

2018 - The 7th Digital Earth Summit 2018, DES-2018, on Digital Earth for Sustainable Development in Africa was to be held in **El Jadida**, Morocco, at the Faculty of Science, Chouaib Douakkali University from April 17-19, 2018.

2019 - The **Santiago** Climate Change Conference, featuring the 25th session of the Conference of the Parties (COP 25) to the United Nations Framework Convention for Climate Change (UNFCCC) and meetings of the UNFCCC subsidiary bodies, convened from 2nd to 13th of December 2019.

2021 - The UK hosted the 26th UN Climate Change Conference of the Parties (COP26) in **Glasgow**, Scotland on 31 October – 13 November 2021.

2022 – Stockholm+50 UN Earth Summit was held in **Stockholm**, Sweden, June 2-3, 2022.

APPENDIX F: List of United Nations Climate Change (UNCC) Conferences

COP stands for "Conference of the Parties."

1   **1995**: COP 1, Berlin, Germany

2   **1996**: COP 2, Geneva, Switzerland

3   **1997**: COP 3, Kyoto, Japan

4   **1998**: COP 4, Buenos Aires, Argentina

5   **1999**: COP 5, Bonn, Germany

6   **2000**: COP 6, The Hague, Netherlands

7   **2001**: COP 6, Bonn, Germany

8 **2001**: COP 7, Marrakech, Morocco

9 **2002**: COP 8, New Delhi, India

10 **2003**: COP 9, Milan, Italy

11 **2004**: COP 10, Buenos Aires, Argentina

12 **2005**: COP 11/CMP 1, Montreal, Canada

13 **2006**: COP 12/CMP 2, Nairobi, Kenya

14 **2007**: COP 13/CMP 3, Bali, Indonesia

15 **2008**: COP 14/CMP 4, Poznań, Poland

16 **2009**: COP 15/CMP 5, Copenhagen, Denmark

17 **2010**: COP 16/CMP 6, Cancún, Mexico

18 **2011**: COP 17/CMP 7, Durban, South Africa

19 **2012**: COP 18/CMP 8, Doha, Qatar

20 **2013**: COP 19/CMP 9, Warsaw, Poland

21 **2014**: COP 20/CMP 10, Lima, Peru

22 **2015**: COP 21/CMP 11, Paris, France

23 **2016**: COP 22/CMP 12/CMA 1, Marrakech, Morocco

24 **2017**: COP 23/CMP 13/CMA 1–2, Bonn, Germany

25 **2018**: COP 24/CMP 14/CMA 1–3, Katowice, Poland

26 **2019**: SB50, Bonn, Germany

27 **2019**: COP 25/CMP 15/CMA 2, Madrid, Spain

28   **2021**: COP 26/CMP 16/CMA 3, Glasgow, United Kingdom

29   **2022**: COP 27, Sharm El Sheikh, Egypt

30   **2023**: COP 28, United Arab Emirates

NOTES

APPENDIX G: List of Major International Climate Protocols

1987 - Montreal Protocol. Signed by every country in the world, banning the use of chemicals like chlorofluorocarbons (CFCs) that damage the ozone layer. In 2016, a Kigali Amendment was added to the protocol, adding hydro-fluorocarbons (HFCs) to the same list.

1992 - UN Framework Convention on Climate Change (UNFCCC). It is the first truly global climate protocol to address the impact of global warming. Ratified by 197 countries, including the United States. It established an annual meeting called *Conference of the Parties (COP)* to facilitate the international discussion of greenhouse gas effects across the globe.

2005 – Kyoto Protocol. Signed by 192 countries, the protocol commits these countries to adopt measures and policies to limit carbon (GHG) emissions in agreement with the individual reduction targets that they agreed to. These targets are binding for 37 industrialized countries who signed the agreement.

2015 – Paris Agreement. It was signed by 196 countries on December 12, 2015, in Paris. The agreement mandated that signatory countries submit **Nationally Determined Contributions** (NDC) for climate action. The United States rejected the agreement during the Trump Administration but rejoined the agreement under President Joe Biden.

SOURCE:

https://unfccc.int/process-and-meetings/the-paris-agreement/the-paris-agreement

(THE END)

NOTES

Printed in Great Britain
by Amazon

14081632R00071